ROCKING
THE CHURCH
MEMBERSHIP
BOAT

ROCKING
THE CHURCH
MEMBERSHIP
BOAT

COUNTING MEMBERS *OR* HAVING MEMBERS WHO COUNT

JAN G. LINN

Chalice Press®
St. Louis, Missouri

Cover illustration: Computer composite of 4th or 5th century mosaic by Michael Domínquez
Cover design: John Grizzell
Interior design: Lynne Condellone
Art direction: Michael Domínguez

This book is printed on acid-free, recycled paper.

Visit Chalice Press on the World Wide Web at
www.chalicepress.com

10 9 8 7 6 5 4 3 2 1   01 02 03 04 05 06

Library of Congress Cataloging–in–Publication Data

Linn, Jan.
    Rocking the church membership boat : counting members or having members who count / Jan G. Linn.
        p.   cm.
    Includes bibliographical references.
        ISBN 0-8272-3224-1 (pbk. : alk paper)
        1. Church membership   I. Title.
    BV820 .L55 2001
    254' .5—dc21   2001000894

Printed in the United States of America

For the community of God's people
called Spirit of Joy

Contents

Acknowledgments   ix

Introduction   1

1. Covenant Membership
   Making Things Better in the Church   7

2. The Percentage Game
   The Way Things Are   29

3. A Brief Excursus
   How Things Got This Way   43

4. Church Shopping
   Making a Bad Situation Worse   49

5. Biblical Reflections
   Testing Membership "Spirits"   57

6. Holding Up Progress
   Personal Obstacles to Covenant Membership   69

7. Privatized Religion
   The Enemy of Covenant Community   79

8. Adaptation
   Stability in a Sea of Change   85

9. Traveling Light
   Proper "Dress" for a Covenant People   97

10. Educating Ministers
    A Covenant Challenge to Seminaries   107

11. Staying in the Church
    Some Personal Reflections   115

12. Questions from Ministers and Laity   121

Notes   139

Acknowledgments

God's grace was at work early in my ministry when, through its Wellspring Mission, I encountered the Church of the Savior in Washington, D. C., and its visionary minister and his wife, Gordon and Mary Cosby. Soon thereafter grace worked again in leading me to a position as a college chaplain, which eventually opened the door to working with Gordon's clergy brothers, P. G. and Beverly, and their faith community, Church of the Covenant, in Lynchburg, Virginia. These model servant leaders first taught me what the church could be when it defined its life and witness by the biblical concept of covenant. That was many years ago, but the passage of time has only confirmed the significance of their influence, which continues to guide my thinking and give me courage when I most need it. I hope this book reflects the best of what I learned from them. At the very least it can serve as a testament of gratitude.

Others have shared more directly in this effort. The last chapter is composed of questions from several clergy colleagues who read the material and raised important issues about the workability of covenant membership in the churches they serve. I express my thanks to them as I describe their assignment at the beginning of that chapter. Here I will simply name them: Loren Olson, Joseph Grubbs, Sotello Long, Cam Holzer, David

Digby, Keith Weekley, Isaac Nicholson, and William McGraw. Their participation in this way has added a special dimension to this book. Thanks also to Joyce Knol Digby, whose careful literary eye added immensely to the quality of this writing.

My wife, Joy, read through every draft and made many suggestions for improvement. As valuable as that was in completing the book, it pales in comparison to her willingness to share the risk of this present ministry. It is grace beyond measure to experience with her daily the sustaining truth that "two are better than one, because they have a good reward for their toil. For if they fall, one will lift up the other" (Eccl. 4:9–10).

Finally, my thanks to Chalice Press for yet another opportunity to work together. Publishing this book allows seeds planted years ago to come to full bloom.

I n the fifth century, monks in Rome gave the
children of the church a symbol for learning
their prayers that was in the shape of arms crossed
over the chest. Its use was later adopted for the
Lenten season in Austria, Germany, and Holland,
and the symbol was sometimes hung on palm
branches as one would decorate a Christmas tree.
This symbol of prayer was the pretzel. In the
nineteenth century it finally made its way to
America and became a commercial success. It is
now looked on as a popular snack food.

Introduction

The title of this book accurately reflects its purpose. Rocking the church membership boat among mainline churches is a call to move from counting members to focusing on having members who count. Many of them have such members already. This book is about how to have more of them. It will not be easy. The underlying conviction of this work is that church membership has lost its biblical bearings and has instead become a good neighbor to the dominant culture, which tries at every turn to corrupt its life and weaken its witness.

It was more than thirty years ago that I first encountered the extent to which the church in America was living in cultural bondage. It was the mid-1960s. I was a theological student serving a church I was not educated for or equipped to serve, but that was the way my denomination did things at the time. Within a few months I began to hear rumors of Saturday night KKK rallies being held in a field not far from our church building. Worse, some of my members were attending. When the fall little league football season arrived, I discovered that the community center sponsoring the team had a "whites only" membership policy. My church members were unapologetic in supporting it, or at best shrugged their shoulders when told about it. That next spring Martin Luther King, Jr., was assassinated. The following Sunday I had a time of silent prayer for the King family as President Johnson had requested of all churches. A man I considered a friend came through the church door after the service, his face burning red and his angry words stinging me as he screamed, "I can't believe you did such a thing for that g*dd*mn communist n*gg*r."

I am sure most of the people thought what he said was profane and wrong. A few even told me they did. But it was no secret that the majority of them were segregationists who belonged to a segregated community center and allowed their children to play on segregated athletic teams. A few of them openly supported the KKK. In short, I was the minister of a church whose members were more Virginian than Christian when it came to racial justice. They were typical of most church members in that community.

I, of course, wanted to quit the ministry. I wasn't even sure I wanted to stay in the church. But Jesus wasn't finished with me. The following Saturday, as I prepared my letter of resignation, God met me in a passage of scripture:

> But we have this treasure in clay jars, so that it may be made clear that this extraordinary power belongs to God and does not come from us. We are afflicted in every way, but not crushed; perplexed, but not driven to despair; persecuted, but not forsaken; struck down, but not destroyed. (2 Cor. 4:7–9)

A wave of emotion overwhelmed me, and I knew deep in my spirit that Jesus had called me into ministry and intended for me to stay. Just as clearly I knew that my congregation's accommodation to a racist culture wasn't going to change quickly, that it was but another example of how all too often the church has come up short when faced with the great moral and ethical issues of every generation. What did change, though, was me. Gone was the naïveté with which I had entered ministry, which had led me to believe the gospel could be clearly heard if honestly preached. Those days taught me the enduring lesson that churches can be their own worst enemy, having eyes that do not see and ears that do not hear because of the influence of the dominant culture around them.

It remains the case today. The difference between now and then is numerical and financial decline. The eyes and ears of mainline churches are no less blurred and no less stopped up when it comes to their relationship to the culture than they were in the 1960s. We see past mistakes but fail to learn from them. This is one of the reasons the book *Resident Aliens,*[1] by Stanley Hauerwas and William Willimon, is such an important book for mainline churches. One note of encouragement is the fact that it has sold more than 50,000 copies, perhaps indicating an emerging awareness of the effects of the church's accommodation to the dominant culture. Hauerwas, of course, is no novice when it comes to stirring the waters among scholars, but with Willimon's help he has his hand in the baptismal font this time. One can hope that churches will not be the same again. But, of course, that will depend on the long-term response of clergy and laity to the book's assault on a liberal Christianity that has convinced people they can be in the church and of the world without compromising the gospel, and on a Christian fundamentalism that rants and raves about a secular culture whose militarism and runaway consumerism it supports.

Yet the book actually spends little time criticizing Christians for being *of* the world. Hauerwas and Willimon know that is only a symptom of the real problem. What's wrong is what I encountered in the 1960s. Churches are not providing much help to their members in knowing how to live in the world with Christian integrity. In many instances, they are bending over backward to blur the lines between culture and church in the hope of building a better society, à la the continuing influence of Richard Niebuhr's "Christ transforming culture"[2] typology of a generation ago. *Resident Aliens* challenges mainline churches to wake up to the dangers of being friends with a dominant culture that possesses the power to turn a simple prayer symbol for children into a profit. Hauerwas and Willimon would say this is nothing more than calling on churches to be the church without apology, timidity, or naïveté.

I believe a major factor that keeps the church from being the church, however, is its easy acceptance of institutionalism as an inevitable result of being in the real world. "You have to have some kind of organization," we say to each other, as if one form of organizing is as good as another. The situation has been made worse by the fact that the dominant culture has convinced churches that organizations must do everything they can to hold on to people so they can maintain institutional needs. The responsibility for "getting people involved" has, of course, fallen on the shoulders of the church's paid staff. As a result they have become "program directors" whose job is to promote the church's agenda. It comes as no surprise that the concept of "resident aliens" strikes many church members today as "alien" to what it takes for a church to make it in the kind of competitive society we live in.

This book argues that it simply is not true that one organizational pattern is as good as another, nor is it true that it is the church's or clergy's job "to get people involved." In my book *The Jesus Connection*[3] I call for a genuine spiritual revival among mainline churches that will be marked by a desire to love Jesus and love the way he loved. In a subsequent work, *Reclaiming Evangelism*,[4] I seek to show that such a spiritual renewal is the key to churches' reclaiming the ministry of evangelism, but that this cannot happen without restructuring the way they are organized. New spirit needs new structure, just as new wine needs a new wineskin. But neither of these books, including the latter, which addresses the matter of structure, confront the one factor in all the talk of renewal of mainline churches (including my own) that is the most critical, controversial, and neglected. It is how people join the church.

This book seeks to fill this void, thus combining with those earlier works to form a kind of trilogy on the renewal of mainline church life. Its genesis was a personal change in ministry. Leaving behind the security of seminary teaching, my wife, Joy, and I responded to the invitation from our denomination to become co-pastors of a new church started in the Twin Cities area of Minnesota. Immediately the question arose as to what kind of church we would be. That in turn forced us to ask what it would mean to belong to the new church. It had been our long-held conviction that *how* people come into the church plays a major role in the level of the commitment they give once they are in.

For this reason we made the decision, with the agreement of the search committee that issued the call to us, to establish a faith community in which people would enter the church through a different door. This book describes what this different door is, why it is so needed, and then seeks to answer questions colleagues have raised about the particulars of this new approach and whether or not it actually offers churches any real help in the renewal effort.

1

Covenant Membership

Making Things Better in the Church

Given the fact that in general a problem is presented before a solution is offered, putting this chapter first might seem akin to having the proverbial cart before the horse. What is more, there are mainline church leaders who are convinced that our worst days are behind us and the future looks bright. If that is the case, this chapter seeks to solve a problem that doesn't exist. But we shall see. For now I have chosen to begin by describing the concept of covenant membership, to which I made passing reference in an earlier work, followed by several chapters that explain why it can change mainline church life.

On some level many people in churches today, especially pastors, know churches need to change the way they approach membership. They know because they have experienced the problems current practices have created, not the least of which is allowing people who are not all that serious about following Jesus not only to join the church but to hold positions of leadership and wield significant influence on a congregation's life and witness. The concept of covenant membership being advocated here will not eliminate these kinds of problems from church life, but *it can and will stop the institutionalizing of them.* This would be a crucial first step in a long process of churches' reasserting their responsibility for defining the biblical meaning of membership in the body of Christ and would mark a turning point in how people currently join the church.

The typical process for becoming a church member in most Protestant churches is for a person to walk down the church aisle, stand before the congregation, and make a profession of faith; they are baptized at that moment or later. In some instances the profession of faith and the baptism are a single act. In general, churches offer membership classes of varying lengths and subject matter, especially for the young. Once someone joins, effort is made to facilitate getting him or her involved through small groups, church school classes, choirs, committees, and so on. But the entire church membership process is largely viewed as not only a personal but a private experience. As one study found:

> Individualism lies at the very core of American culture… We believe in the dignity, indeed the sacredness, of the individual. Anything that would violate our right to think for ourselves, judge for ourselves, make our own decisions, live our lives as we see fit, is not only morally wrong, it is sacrilegious.[5]

In the area of religious experience the study concludes that most Americans believe "an individual should arrive at his or her own religious beliefs independent of any churches or synagogues."[6]

Current membership practices in most mainline churches are an extension of this kind of privatized religion. This is why covenant membership requires a new way of thinking altogether. It calls for viewing church membership as a *spiritual discipline.* The biblical basis for this perspective is the fact that membership in the body of Christ means loving Jesus and loving the way Jesus loves. It is at least presumptuous to think anyone joins the church already capable of either understanding the implications of this dual challenge or living by it. We may be "born again," but we are certainly not born full grown into being connected to Jesus. Membership, then, by its very nature, ought to be understood as a process of spiritual maturing. If joining the church means anything, it must mean we have made the decision to commit ourselves to becoming disciplined in spiritual growth and development.

From this point of view, membership takes on a dynamic character in contradistinction to the traditional approach, which is essentially passive. As a spiritual discipline, church membership becomes work a person does for the purpose of spiritual growth. Spiritual disciplines require effort because they are not ends but means, pointing us toward the spiritual goals of loving Jesus and loving the way he loved.

The Latin root of the word *discipline* means training or instruction that molds or perfects a specific skill. To think of church membership as a spiritual discipline would mean viewing it as a way to train for or gain instruction in the life of the Spirit, to become spiritually mature as athletes become mature in their particular sport or field. Training or instruction sometimes involves doing it when you don't feel like it, when you don't have the energy or time or determination to continue. In short, that which is a discipline, spiritual or otherwise, requires a conscious choice on a regular basis to maintain it.

Church membership as a spiritual discipline has three primary goals. The first is *to grow stronger in one's faith in Jesus as Savior*. The gospel of John declares Jesus to be God in the flesh: "And the Word became flesh and lived among us, and we have seen his glory, the glory as of a father's only son, full of grace and truth" (1:14). The text means God pitched a tent among human beings in the person of Jesus of Nazareth. In various ways this is the proclamation of the New Testament. Jesus is Christ, Messiah, the Son of God, God in the flesh, God in human form, God with us in a dynamic, intimate way, God in Christ reconciling the world to God's self.

But faith in Jesus as Savior also means affirming him to be raised from the dead. It is, as Luke Timothy Johnson points out, thinking of Jesus as alive rather than thinking of Jesus as dead, which makes all the difference in the way we think about him and about ourselves.[7] The New Testament message is not simply that Jesus lived. It is that he lives. It is a message about his crucifixion only because he was raised from the dead. The apostle Paul pointed to the resurrection as the cornerstone of Christian faith when he wrote:

> For I handed on to you as of first importance what I in turn had received: that Christ died for our sins in accordance with the scriptures, and that he was buried, and that he was raised on the third day in accordance with the scriptures…
>
> Now if Christ is proclaimed as raised from the dead, how can some of you say there is no resurrection of the dead? If there is no resurrection of the dead, then Christ has not been raised; and if Christ has not been raised, then our proclamation has been in vain and your faith has been in vain. We are even found to be misrepresenting God, because we testified of God that he raised Christ—whom he did not raise if it is true that the dead are not raised. For if the dead are not raised, then Christ has not been raised. If Christ has not been raised, your faith is futile and you are still in your sins. Then those also who have died in Christ have perished. If for this life only we have hoped in Christ, we are of all people most to be pitied.
>
> But in fact Christ has been raised from the dead, the first fruits of those who have died. (1 Cor. 15:3,12–20)

Church membership begins with the affirmation of one's faith in the truth of this message. It is a symbol of one's recognition that membership is about giving rather than getting because we who choose to belong have already received all we will ever need in Jesus Christ, and far more than we could ever deserve. At the same time, because it is a spiritual discipline, it also helps us grow in faith, thus heeding Jesus' words, "Not everyone who says to me, 'Lord, Lord,' will enter the kingdom of heaven, but only the one who does the will of my Father in heaven" (Mt. 7:21). Membership as a spiritual discipline recognizes that no one can claim to do "the will of [the] Father in heaven" perfectly, or even well. Growth, therefore, is the goal in order for faith in Jesus as Savior to make any practical difference.

The second goal is *to love Jesus.* This is a step beyond belief. Belief positions us to take this step, but it cannot be a substitute for it. The mystical dimension of church membership is experiencing the reality of being part of the body of Christ. The doorway to this experience is love. It is what Jesus wants from us more than anything else: "When they had finished breakfast, Jesus said to Simon Peter, 'Simon, son of John, do you love me more than these?'" (Jn. 21:15). It was the last question Jesus asked his disciples. Do you love me? It is the question church membership answers, and at the same time strengthens.

Not everything about loving Jesus is mystical. Loving includes the mind as well as heart. Yet the heart is the root of devotion and keeps us in the church when understanding eludes us. At times I have stayed in ministry because of the mystical reality of the presence of Jesus and my desire to love him first in my life, even though the circumstances around me cried out for me to give up, and logic seemed to suggest this was a foolish and futile way to spend one's life.

Opening the heart to Jesus is, I believe, much harder for mainline Christians than is intellectual assent to the gospel. Schooled in rationalism, and suspicious of emotionalism, many have come to faith "kicking and screaming," what with the illogic of believing a dead man was raised to live again. To go another step and love this One we cannot see, but whose presence we are told we can "experience," asks much of us and stretches us in uncomfortable ways. But this is simply an argument for membership as a spiritual discipline that teaches us that obedience is a way of "listening" to truth, opening us to an experience of reality neither knowledge nor logic can explain or explain away. Membership, then, is a commitment to grow into loving Jesus.

The final goal of church membership is *witnessing through love,* which is a basic challenge Jesus himself puts before us: "I give you a new commandment, that you love one another. Just as I have loved you, you also should love one another. By this everyone will know that you are my disciples, if you have love for one another" (Jn. 13:34–35). It is loving the way Jesus loved, love expressed in actions as well as words. It is the sine qua non of church membership. Joining the church is a sign of both our desire to witness through love and our need for this desire to be nurtured.

These three goals are, of course, intertwined and dependent on one another. They are of a piece, and it is called discipleship. That is what church membership is—the sign of Christian discipleship and the means by which it grows.

Covenant membership in the church is not only grounded in these goals, but also defines those things that can help church members reach them. It is an intentional binding together of two or more people in a relationship of mutual support and responsibility. Put simply, a covenant is a promise made and a promise kept. Covenant membership defines that promise. Its effectiveness depends on being both *specific* and *unambiguous.* *Specific* means explicitly set forth, not general, distinctive, even unique. A covenant membership statement would avoid being platitudinous so as not to obscure the meaning and leave members on their own to determine what the statement means for them in actual practice.

Ambiguous means having two or more possible meanings or interpretations, being vague, unclear, uncertain. The Latin root means to wander about, to move from side to side, or to be indecisive. *Unambiguous,* then, means the opposite of these—having only one meaning or interpretation, clear, certain, understandable, decisive.

The most widely known covenant pledge people make today is the marriage vow. Marriage rests on promises made and promises kept, promises that are specific and unambiguous. "To love, honor, and cherish for as long as we both shall live." Nothing unclear or equivocating about that. It is a model for covenant membership in the church. Churches help members in faithfulness to God, one another, and themselves by making expectations specific and unambiguous.

At Spirit of Joy we have chosen to use the following covenant membership statement:

> By God's grace given in and through Jesus Christ, whom I have confessed as Savior and Lord of my life, I joyfully commit myself to being a member of the Spirit of Joy T.E.A.M. This means for this year I am willing to give my *time* in attendance, my *energy* in ministry, my *attention* in prayer, and my *money* in support, all to the building up of this community of faith and its witness to Jesus Christ in the world.
>
> In making this covenant I am consciously pledging to love and serve the Lord, and to trust the Holy Spirit to lead me in all things to witness to my faith through word and deed.
>
> If there should be times when I feel like I am being stretched in uncomfortable ways, I will also trust the Spirit to use them to nudge me toward deeper spiritual maturity.
>
> May God bless me and all who share in this covenant, that together we may be a blessing to others. Amen.

Each statement of the covenant was thought through carefully to convey the commitment, support, and power that membership in the church can have. Time, energy, attention, and money. These are words people understand. We know them through home and work. At Spirit of Joy we believe they are words that appropriately describe what it means to be a member of the church because they embody the commandments to love God with all our heart, soul, mind, and strength and to love our neighbors as ourselves.

TIME

"I am willing to give my time *in attendance..."*

People have to be present in a church to be involved. As obvious as that sounds, more than a few members of churches apparently think otherwise. We do not accept such an attitude. A commitment of time in attendance is the essential—in fact, foundational—element of church life. Without this commitment, membership has little meaning or integrity.

For us, worship is the first place this happens. It is the primary means of spiritual growth and nurture, but it also is a regular confession that we acknowledge God alone as sovereign and holy. Attending worship is a public statement of our need for God. It is also a way of saying we care enough about one another to be present. In community, people have to be present to be nurtured and nurture others. They have to be present to give and receive love. Relationships require presence. We are simply stating the obvious when we say we expect members to be present. That takes time.

Time is one of the precious gifts we often take for granted. My father died one year after my family and I moved back to my hometown, where I had not lived since leaving for college. How often I have wished I had had more time to get to know him as his adult son, really know him. It didn't occur to me I wouldn't until he died. Then it was too late.

We talk about time in such careless ways. "Killing time," "marking time," "wasting time," "spending time"—all common statements. At least "time is money" underscores the value of time. The one thing all of us should know about time is that we don't have enough of it. That is why priorities become the factor that determines how we "use" time. Making a time commitment of attending worship a part of our covenant membership statement is our way of saying that devoting time to God in praise and worship in community is not accidental or coincidental. It is a priority. Stating it openly confronts all of us with the reality that attending worship is not something we do when nothing else gets in the way. It is a choice that involves not doing other things we could do.

This is important, because weekly worship attendance is viewed by many church members as something that is good but not integral to their spiritual well-being. Certainly there are times when absence from worship is unavoidable and understandable. The issue covenant membership confronts is the temptation to be absent from worship because of misplaced priorities. Every church has people it can count on to be present on Sunday morning, and when they are not, everyone knows there is a serious reason. These people have already made a covenant with God and the church to give their time in attendance, and are seldom resistant to saying so openly through the use of a covenant statement. It's the people who haven't made this kind of inward covenant who question a covenant membership statement. Ironically, they are the very ones who need it the most, because they are the ones who tend to want to make membership solely a private matter. Would that every church member were to commit to memory the words of Oswald Chambers, who once wrote, "There is no other time than now with God, no past and no future."[8] A Sunday not spent in worship with one's church family is a Sunday lost forever.

But time is about more than presence. It is really a matter of preparedness—at least that is what Jesus seems to be saying in his parable of the ten bridesmaids (Mt. 25:1–13). All ten were waiting for the bridegroom to appear for the wedding to start, but only five had sufficient oil in their lamps for the long delay. The lamps of the other five ran low, so they left to get more oil. While they were gone, the bridegroom came and the wedding party went inside. Upon their return they discovered they were locked out, and the bridegroom would not let them in because they had not been prepared for his coming.

That is the way it is with Jesus. He expects us to be prepared at all times for his coming, for his call, for his Spirit, leading us into his work. Worship is the most essential "wedding feast" the church holds. It is the cornerstone for everything else. Those who neglect it cannot possibly be well equipped to love and serve the Lord. That is why in our covenant membership a commitment of time in attendance in worship is not optional.

ENERGY
"my energy in ministry..."

Many people feel like the man who jumped on a horse and rode off in every direction. Schedules are packed full of activities that are mentally and physically draining. A family meal around the table at home has become a rarity. In many households breakfast is the most likely time when a meal together might happen, but even then it often becomes little more than family members rotating in and out. Adults and kids today are tired, weary from the pace of life they have created for themselves.

In the midst of this, the church has no choice but to tell members that it requires energy to keep the pace individuals and families live today and also join with others in ministry. Covenant membership confronts this fact with the conviction that the key to energy is ministry with deep spiritual roots that becomes a reservoir of life and energy. This connects membership with ministry in that we ask people to serve where they sense a call rather than on a committee. Some people may be energized by serving on church committees, but the pattern of poor attendance suggests their numbers are few. Ministries are different because they are born from people serving out of call rather than persuasion or election. Add to that the focus on serving through the use of one's spiritual gifts, and it is not difficult to see how people give and receive energy in ministry at Spirit of Joy.

At the same time, it takes personal discipline to get involved. There will always be times when a member of a ministry would rather not go to the meeting. That is the reason for the covenant. Self-discipline to do what one feels too weary to do is strengthened simply by the fact that one has made a commitment to others. Every team athlete knows this to be true. You "grind it out," see what you're made of, so to speak, not when the adrenaline is flowing, but when you feel as if you cannot go another step.

Church members face this kind of challenge once they commit themselves to a specific ministry. A covenant statement can help, because it reminds all members they have made a commitment to one another. Not to honor that commitment hurts the group. A promise made in the church should be a promise kept. Our covenant membership statement seeks to be explicit in holding people to their word. A biblical basis for doing so is the words of Jesus to the man who wanted to go bury his father before following Jesus: "No one who puts a hand to the plow and looks back is fit for the kingdom of God" (Lk. 9:62).

The enemy of this kind of commitment of energy to the church's ministry is volunteerism. Most people see all voluntary service as optional, even in the church. Any minister is grateful for church members who serve without pause or hesitation because they are always ready to volunteer. But covenant membership challenges doing the work of the church this way out of the conviction, based on experience, that volunteerism is no friend to commitment. As such, it unequivocally declares that serving in ministry is not optional for those who claim membership in Christ's church. More important, though, is the fact that new members of ministry groups are energized by high commitment expectations.

ATTENTION
"my attention *in prayer..."*

Martin Luther once wrote that Christians should pray for thirty minutes a day, and if they are really busy, they should pray for an hour. It was his way of saying that, just as with other aspects of our covenant statement, prayer is not optional.

The truth is, attention to prayer is self-authenticating, yet it is one of the most neglected parts of Christian living today. People may say they pray daily in public surveys, but personal conversations contradict such findings, suggesting that they not only don't pray but don't tell the truth about it. Churches need to be open and candid in expecting members to pray. At Spirit of Joy we often say a church that does not pray is a church not to be trusted. The same can be said of ministries. Every ministry should be grounded in the life of prayer and guided and empowered by the Holy Spirit.

One of the problems church members have with praying on a regular basis is not believing they know how. One of our participants said as much to me after a sermon on prayer. It was an honest request for help. Our response has been to create spiritual life groups and retreat opportunities that teach people about prayer. We also preach about the power and practice of prayer and focus on various types of praying during corporate worship. Covenant membership trusts the biblical promise that the Spirit will pray on our behalf if we simply make the effort:

> Likewise the Spirit helps us in our weakness; for we do not know how to pray as we ought, but that very Spirit intercedes with sighs too deep for words. And God, who searches the heart, knows what is the mind of the Spirit, because the Spirit intercedes for the saints according to the will of God. (Rom. 8:26–27)

But our concern goes beyond individual prayer. Our intention is for the church as a body to attend to its collective need for prayer. This is why ministries worship together and share in discussion time the common struggles and triumphs that go with praying. Our goal is that every group, as well as the community's corporate worship life, witness to the need for prayer. This way the church practices what it preaches about individual prayer.

One church that has understood the centrality of corporate prayer for its life and ministry is the Brooklyn Tabernacle. The pastor, Jim Cymbala, writes candidly about the need for and lack of prayer in churches:

> Let's not play games with ourselves. Let's not divert attention away from the weak prayer of our churches.

In Acts 4, when the apostles were unjustly arrested, imprisoned, and threatened, they didn't call for a protest; they didn't reach for some political leverage. Instead, they headed to a prayer meeting. Soon the place was vibrating with the power of the Holy Spirit.[9]

When he asks what will turn the tide against people destroying their lives with drugs and alcohol and sexual promiscuity, he once again appeals to the ministry of prayer.

Preaching alone will not do it; classes aren't going to do it; more money for more programs won't do it. Only turning God's house into a house of fervent prayer will reverse the power of evil so evident in the world today.[10]

Brooklyn Tabernacle has a ministry of prayer called the Prayer Band. These are folks who participate in a prayer chain that prays twenty-four hours a day, seven days a week, all year round. They pray for the worship services while they are in progress. Jim Cymbala believes that without this kind of commitment to prayer the Tabernacle would not have the ministry it has.

But, of course, it's not a mainline church. As one woman asked me when I made reference to the church in a lecture, "They lean toward being Pentecostal, don't they?" She was exactly right! They are Pentecostal. They are also a picture of the "rainbow coalition" membership the rest of us only talk about, multiracial and multicultural. In addition, more than a few of the members came into the tabernacle right off the street, where they were wasting away doing crack cocaine and heroin or being consumed by addictions to alcohol and illicit sex.

Brooklyn Tabernacle has never been afraid to confront people with the church's expectations for membership. One story that stands out is about an unmarried young couple who were living together when they came forward to confess Christ and join the church. On learning of their living arrangement, Jim Cymbala told them with pastoral sensitivity and honesty that living together outside of marriage was considered willful sinning by the church. He asked them to go home and pray to see if they could follow God, who would lead them to a different view of life. A few weeks later the couple returned with the news that they had decided to live separately until they were able to be married. They were then received into the church as members.[11]

We may have a different view of this issue, but for our discussion the point to note is that this church and minister are willing to hold to a standard they believe in, even at the risk of losing a young couple ready to join. Apparently this approach has not limited numerical growth. The Brooklyn Tabernacle, located in what would be labeled a "non-growth" area, has grown from fifteen people to more than six thousand and is now busy starting new churches. It is a ministry grounded in individual and corporate prayer. They reject the use of marketing techniques for numerical growth. Instead they rely on preaching the gospel as they understand it, being a people of prayer, and trusting their future to the work and power of the Holy Spirit.

At Spirit of Joy we have begun a time of prayer among those leading JoyLand Ministry for children and those leading worship. Each week we gather twice for prayer before each ministry begins. We also invite anyone else in the congregation to join the circle of prayer as a way to witness to the need for corporate prayer to undergird ministry.

As a starting point for beginners in prayer we have developed what we call the three-step spiritual growth exercise: (1) Commit the day to Jesus before it gets going; (2) Recommit the day to him at noon; (3) Thank Jesus for being present during the day before going to sleep. The exercise is patterned after the traditional Jesus Prayer ("Lord, Jesus, have mercy on me, a sinner"), which is to be repeated several times a day. Our goal is to learn how, on a daily basis, to depend on God personally and as a community of faith. For this to happen we have to trust ourselves to God. This means we have to be conscious of God. We have learned by experience that the three-step exercise helps in both ways. Even for those of us who pray on a regular basis, this exercise increases our sense of the presence of God in our lives, which, of course, is the purpose for taking the time to pray in the first place.

MONEY
"and my money *in support..."*

In a book I wrote I juxtaposed two chapters about money and the church to make the point we try to emphasize at Spirit of Joy. One chapter was titled "The Church Wants More Than Your Money." The second was "The Church Wants Your Money Too."[12] Our covenant membership statement seeks to embody this way of thinking. The commitment we expect of time, energy, and attention says the church wants more than people's money. Churches want people before they get anything from them. But money is also part of church membership. We want members to know this.

The issue of money can create controversy in churches. Some people claim that all the church talks about is money. Others think it doesn't talk about it enough. A colleague recently brought to his church's attention the fact that only a few years ago they sent out pledge cards for members to fill out. Now they send out "Estimates of Giving" cards, indicative of a subtle but significant change in the way the church approaches the matter of money.

Perhaps some of this problem stems from the fact that scripture seems to take an ambivalent approach to the subject. Throughout the Bible are warnings of the dangers of money. Ecclesiastes, for example, says, "The lover of money will not be satisfied with money; nor the lover of wealth, with gain" (5:10). When Jesus tells the rich ruler to sell everything and then come and follow him (Mt. 19:21), he turns the wisdom writer's admonition into a warning about the power of money standing between us and following Jesus. Other examples of this view of money are to be found.

But other texts highlight the positive potential of money. In the parable of the talents, the men who multiplied their wealth were commended for good stewardship, while the man with the smallest amount was condemned for not doing the same thing (Mt. 25:14–30). He tried to play it safe and lost. The message is clear. God expects us to use our resources wisely, whether they be money or abilities.

This is the point we are making with this part of our covenant membership statement. Churches are at ease talking about people using their talents and abilities to support the church. We think money should be included.

Currently we do not pass an offering plate during worship at Spirit of Joy. Instead we place an offering box on a table in the back of the worship area. Verbally and in written messages in the bulletin we emphasize the need and importance of financial support for our ministry. As we grow, this practice may change to offering baskets being passed through the aisles, but, for now, asking people to make the effort to seek out the offering box seems to make the point that giving money to the church is an expectation of membership.

One of the things we have discovered in working with unchurched people is that they honestly do not know how to get started in being good financial stewards as part of their commitment to covenant membership. One young woman asked recently what we meant when we talked about a "tithe." She wanted to know what you do if you are already too financially strapped to give a tenth of your income. She also needed guidance about whether a tithe is based on gross or net income. These are practical questions that need to be answered to help members become financially responsible to the church. So we told her to start with a percentage that was realistic for her budget the first year, and then increase it each year thereafter to reach a tithe. We also suggested she use net income as a basis for the percentage, then tithe on any tax refund she receives. The important thing is to be regular in one's giving, we said, and to be determined to expand it. When money is given regularly, it doesn't take long to discover that what loomed as a strain on the family budget turns out to be much easier than anticipated.

Our goal is for our people to understand that money need not be a "hushed" topic in the church, but can be discussed openly. Even more, though, we want them to experience financial stewardship as an essential element of spiritual growth. Theologian Douglas John Hall says stewardship is not part of the Christian mission, it *is* the Christian mission.[13] We are convinced that making money a part of covenant commitment will have the effect of helping church members gain a broader understanding of stewardship. Then they will see that the other aspects of our covenant statement also speak of stewardship. So we talk about money without embarrassment or hesitation. We are free with information about how the church spends the money it receives. Once we grow into a Ministry Council composed of representatives from the various ministries, we will allocate a yearly amount, but leave it to the council's discretion to allocate it on a monthly basis. Each ministry will then present proposals to the council to receive financial support.

All this is an intentional way to focus on the fact that membership involves a financial commitment to the church's life and ministry. It takes money to establish and support a church's ministry. That means members have to give. But this commitment adds up to a lot more than money. The act of contributing to ministry positions members to experience the spiritual inspiration of seeing their faith in action. When kids return from church camp so excited about the experience they can hardly keep themselves on the ground, all because their church made it financially possible for them to go, members experience money as something much more than a covenant obligation. This kind of experience is repeated again and again when churches do not hesitate to make financial support an expectation for membership. That is why we have made it an element of our covenant statement.

Unity and Diversity

An essential dimension of the covenant is the statement alluding to a commitment to be a positive force in the life of the church:

> ...all to the building up of this community of faith and its witness to Jesus Christ in the world.

Making this expectation part of the covenant has the power of bringing into focus the need for commitment to the health and well-being of the whole. To anyone who wants to join Spirit of Joy the covenant says that we expect you to help us become stronger, that exercising your spiritual gift is intended for the good of all. In this regard we are reflecting the counsel of the apostle Paul when he wrote to the Christians at Corinth and Ephesus:

> To each is given the manifestation of the Spirit for the common good. (1 Cor. 12:7)

> The gifts he gave were that some would be apostles, some prophets, some evangelists, some pastors and teachers, to equip the saints for the work of ministry, for building up the body of Christ, until all of us come to the unity of the faith and of the knowledge of the Son of God, to maturity, to the measure of the full stature of Christ. (Eph. 4:11–13)

> Let no evil talk come out of your mouths, but only what is useful for building up, as there is need, so that your words may give grace to those who hear. (Eph. 4:29)

This aspect of our covenant highlights the communal dimension of church membership, intentionally contrasting the individualism of the dominant culture. We want every member to know she has the power in word and deed to build up or tear down our life together.

For members to build up, they must be willing "to be stretched in uncomfortable ways," as our covenant also states. Differences in views, understandings, and perspectives are part of community life. Too often they become a basis for divisions. At Spirit of Joy we have no desire for everyone to think or act the same way. Quite the opposite. The covenant seeks to affirm the place for differences so long as they are used to build up rather than tear down. It is a common experience in church life today for this not to be the case. The covenant provides us with a way to make unity an expectation while encouraging and nurturing diversity.

Witness

Our covenant concludes with an emphasis on the "witnessing" aspect of church membership.

In making this covenant I am consciously pledging to love and serve the Lord, and to trust the Holy Spirit to lead me in all things to witness to my faith through word and deed.

We believe church membership means committing one's self to fulfilling the great commission in daily life. Witnessing is not optional for members of the church. It is who they are and what they do all the time. The point we are making in this section of the statement is that making covenant itself is a witnessing act and that being a covenant community is the way we fulfill the great commission as a church. We believe evangelism is more than an individual responsibility, that it involves a corporate witness. Our witness is not limited to personal integrity as individual Christians. Covenant membership is our witness as members of the body of Christ called Spirit of Joy.

Accountability

One of the difficulties of the covenant membership approach is the issue of *accountability*. In other words, is there any process for confronting the problem of covenant breaking? For most mainline Protestant churches, which have virtually no authority of any kind, there is no simple answer. But it helps to know in precise terms what accountability is. The word *accountable* means "obliged to answer for one's actions." The root word for *account* means "to make good use of" or "to reckon." Being accountable simply means putting one's self in the position of being held responsible for the commitments one makes. Rather than being an intrusion on individual rights, accountability is a positive action. It is a practical way of saying to others that we will live up to our promises and do our part in helping them. It also invites them to help us keep our word.

This aspect of accountability—mutual support—has unfortunately become a casualty of people's resistance to loyalty to anything beyond one's own interests. But the church is called to be an alternative community to radical individualism. We are the body of Christ, and holding one another accountable for commitments made is the way we *help one another* stay a healthy functioning member of the body.

But how does accountability work out practically? How does a church hold members accountable for the covenant they make with one another? The ideal would be for all to say on a regular basis whether or not they are living up to their promises. One church has members write what they call a "spiritual report" in which they do this. In a class I taught in spiritual formation I had my students turn in such a report on a weekly basis, with the caveat that it was intended to be a way for them to share what was happening to them on their spiritual journey, anything they were comfortable sharing. As they wrote they could include whether or not they were practicing their prayer disciplines. I then wrote comments in the margins and returned them.

Students found this to be a helpful practice. At times it served as a means of confession that they had not been praying. With others it was a way to share the joy of what was happening to them, along with some of the struggles they were encoun-tering. My role in commenting on these reports was to offer encouragement and suggestions for things they could try to help them with a problem they were having. The reports were always cautious in content at the beginning of the semester, but they quickly moved to open and honest sharing of thoughts and feelings.

I was in a position to make this a requirement of the class members. I have no doubt that ministers expecting this of members would meet with cries for their removal. But I have often thought it a great loss to the church that something years of experience have shown to be a valuable tool for helping people grow spiritually would be rejected without comment by the majority of church members.

One of the ways we have approached accountability is through verbal sharing in ministry and spiritual life groups. Once people become comfortable with one another, they begin to share at a level most of them would not have expected. One thing that sets them at ease is that they discover they are not alone in the questions, doubts, and struggles they have. They experience the truth about being in the body of Christ, as the apostle Paul identified, "for whenever I am weak, then I am strong" (2 Cor. 12:10).

One of the important ways we are working with the need for accountability is by making *our covenant membership an annual commitment.* Worship is the appropriate context for this act. An annual covenant renewal service can revolutionize the way people think about membership. It is a forthright witness to the need for constant renewal of one's baptismal vows. The fact that it is done in community adds to both the significance and power of recommitment.

There is, of course, a risk involved. Some people may choose not to renew their membership vows. But the freedom to make this choice annually will have the effect of making all commitments that much stronger. Annual commitment allows people to move in and out of membership as they determine whether or not they are ready to live by the membership covenant. The option to say no underscores that membership in the church is an important decision, and invites them to reclaim the yes they spoke a year earlier.

Annual commitment is a step any church can take without much pain. Members who already view membership as discipleship can immediately embrace it. Those stuck in institutional thinking will be challenged to stretch without being forced into it. This allows people to experience the value of covenant membership without the pressure that if they do not, they will be removed from the church roll. One congregation has made it voluntary for existing members but a requirement for all new members.

Covenant membership offers established churches a communal way to highlight the serious nature of membership without having to fight the battle of taking names off the roll. More important, it changes the focus from institutional maintenance to faithfulness and becomes a deterrent to people thinking nominal membership is an option when joining. By its very nature it respects the freedom to be a participant without commitment while protecting the integrity of membership. In this way, joining the church becomes a decision to enter the church through a different door into a community offering an alternative to the dominant culture.

Covenant membership can have a dramatic effect on church life because it is a practical way to begin reestablishing the integrity of the church's witness. By counting as members only those who annually declare their intention to love and serve the Lord, it automatically limits the potential for nominal commitment.

To be sure, there is no perfect membership in the church, because there are no perfect people to live it out. But covenant membership offers a way to do better. At the very least, it is a step in the right direction.

2

The Percentage Game

The Way Things Are

Some ministers and church members may worry that covenant membership throws a desire for numerical growth out the window. It does not. It simply shifts attention away from numerical growth and onto the integrity of church membership. If the desire for numerical growth can be approached within the context of covenant membership, churches will have much to gain and nothing to lose. A personal story will help to make this point.

My father spent part of his boyhood years in a Presbyterian orphanage, where he was baptized into the church. It wasn't something about which he had much to say or anything to which he devoted much thought. As an adult he chose not to attend church, but my mother took my brothers and me every week. Ours was a church that not only practiced immersion as the only form of baptism but went even further and required re-baptism of all nonimmersed persons.

A grand and wonderful man named George Dalton, who was superintendent of the Sunday school, which had a weekly average attendance of nearly two thousand, took a special interest in my Dad's joining the church. His goal was to get him to attend, but he decided the way to do it would be to get him to join first. That meant Dad had to be re-baptized. It was not something he "warmed to." He saw no reason for it, since he had already been baptized. Being a persistent man without being offensive, Mr. Dalton stayed on Dad's trail until Dad finally gave up and gave in. The family always thought the fact that Mr. Dalton was a Roosevelt Democrat played a major role in Dad's decision, but he never said so. Anyway, the day arrived for the re-baptism. Actually it took place just prior to the Sunday night worship service, which was the general practice in our church at the time. Mother, my two brothers, and I watched anxiously as Dad came down the steps to meet our minister, Dr. John Suttenfield, who had also played no small role in getting him to this point. Dr. Suttenfield asked Dad to reaffirm his acceptance of Jesus Christ as the Son of God and his personal Savior and then he laid him back into the water and raised him up to new life. At least that's what it symbolized.

As the worship service began, we expected Dad to join us. It didn't happen. As time passed, Mother grew more and more anxious. By the end she was beside herself and wasted no time getting my brothers and me down the street to our house, where we found Dad sitting in his easy chair watching television. When Mother asked him why he hadn't come to worship, he replied without hesitation, "*Bonanza* was on."

This story illustrates what is wrong with church growth under current standards for membership. Change the context to covenant membership, and the story would be very different. Either Dad would not have joined or he would not have gone home to watch his favorite television show. Covenant membership would have expected more and, not getting it, would have forced him to make a decision within the year about how serious he really was about Christian discipleship. (I am glad to say that later in his life he made the decision to become a "real" member of the church.)

One might hope the intrinsic appeal of covenant membership would make ministers and churches embrace it without hesitation. But if a minister friend's experience is any guide, that is unlikely to happen. He said that when he floated the idea among his people, they saw it as a threat to a treasured way of life. His experience suggests that making a compelling case for covenant membership is a formidable challenge.

An experience of a former seminary colleague of mine also supports this suspicion. He spoke at a large gathering of congregations. He had spent a number of years as a congregational pastor before joining the faculty. He cares deeply about the church and its witness in the world. For this reason he spoke at length and with candor about the current state of mainline churches, their decline, struggles, and challenges, and spiritual anemia, ending with what he believed was a note of hope grounded in the gospel. Soon after returning home, he received an angry letter from a minister who attended the meeting. He said he was tired of hearing about how bad things were in the church and how it is in decline. He considered this friend's preaching a voice of doom the church could do without.

The minister who wrote the letter is pastor of a numerically growing church that left its downtown location to catch the wave of growth its current suburban location is experiencing. It lists a membership of more than 1,600. Of this number, it counts 1,000 as actual participants.[14] But the weekly worship attendance is only slightly more than half that number. This means that, of the total membership the church claims, only about one fourth actually show up for worship on a given Sunday. Yet this man believes good things are happening in the church.

Others view church life from the same perspective. They believe religion in America is "riding high in the saddle," so to speak, and churches are once again beginning to reap the reward. It is one point of view, of course, except that no reliable statistics support it. More important, though, it reveals a particular and, in my opinion, disconcerting attitude about church membership, which is, *church membership is a percentage game.* It goes like this: You get as many people as possible to join in the hope that a sufficient number will attend and give some money. This approach is considered one of facing reality. Not everyone is going to make a genuine commitment to the church, so you have to play the percentages. This may be a more candid way of stating the matter than those of this persuasion are wont to do, but it fairly and accurately reflects the essence of their view of church membership.

Because "you win some and lose some" in this approach, how new members are assimilated becomes an important consideration. "Ease the path as much as possible," Joy and I were told, "then try to get people involved." In the real world, it takes people and money to make a church go. Get them any way you can because that's what it takes in the kind of competitive world we live in. If you don't, somebody else will. Make them feel a part of something right away. Slow down the process and you'll lose them. It's a matter of economic survival. Get them in, then try to do something with them.

This is the path to membership in most churches. Joining is not a very difficult process. For the unbaptized, in denominations like my own it can take as little as a couple of weeks. Some ministers take professions of faith on the spot, followed immediately by baptism. Switching from one church to another is virtually instantaneous. The fact is, the church is one of the easiest organizations around to join.

But let's examine carefully where this way of doing church membership has gotten us. Consider again the church served by the minister who wrote my former colleague the angry letter. As we noted, a little more than one fourth of the people who are members actually attend. Almost half of them are not even considered active by the church itself.

There are other examples of this pattern. One church generally considered as the most prestigious pulpit in its denomination boasts of a membership exceeding 3,000, with 2,100 counted as "participating." The average weekly worship attendance is 845, which is less than 30 percent of the total membership the church reports. Another one is a church that qualifies for the title "megachurch" with a membership of more than 8,500. It reports 7,500 in the "participating" category, but its average weekly attendance is 3,500.

The same pattern is found even among new churches. A six-year-old congregation reports a membership of 137, with 115 participating, but a weekly average of 72. A very large church about ten years old has a membership of 3,346, with 2,500 "participating," but only 900 for an average worship attendance. Percentages in a third church that is about the same age fare better, with a membership of 185, with 165 "participating," and a worship attendance of 137, but the trend is similar to the others.

All this is even more remarkable when one considers that the threshold for membership and even "participating" membership in these churches is hardly challenging, as well as the fact that as a rule churches report the highest possible figures they can send in to their denominational headquarters. It comes as no surprise to learn that all denominational statistics show the same pattern of their congregations. My tradition, for example, reports slightly more than 853,000 in total membership. Approximately 550,000 fall into the "participating" category, and of that group less than 300,000 actually attend weekly worship.[15] Thus, overall denominational percentages parallel those of most congregations. But the story could actually be worse than it appears to be, even if we factor in homebound and nursing home members who genuinely love the Lord and continue to support the church in ways available to them. The figures for the total and participating membership categories include estimates for non-reporting congregations. Membership estimates are notoriously inflated in churches, so chances are that actual figures are below those reported.

Although the categories for reporting may vary, the discrepancies between membership and actual worship attendance is not peculiar to any single mainline denomination. A modest conclusion one can draw from this statistical analysis is that *the way mainline churches do membership is not working very well.* When only about one fourth of the people who join the church actually attend worship, that alone should be sufficient reason to reassess what is going on with the way churches approach membership. Yet this doesn't seem to be the case. Instead, the focus continues to be on what can be done to turn around total membership decline.

The reason is simple: *Church membership has become institutionalized.* The result has been the loss of membership integrity. Churches have become enculturated to the point that they can no longer define the meaning of membership. The effects are often subtle, and too easily dismissed. Consider the following:

"He actually raises his arm in the air and points at his watch if the worship service runs overtime." The minister who was telling me this said that if the service went five minutes past noon, this man, who holds a Ph.D. in psychology, would throw up his arm with his finger pointing to the watch.

One might think—or even wish—this man was a troubled soul who wasn't in full control of himself to explain his rudeness. But the truth is, though most people are not so crude as he, his actions represent the attitude many church members have about worship these days. At least in white churches. African American congregations don't have this problem, but predominately white churches do. We live by the clock. Every minister is compelled to preach the eternal gospel ever conscious of minutes.

It is a common experience for ministers, this pressure to make sure worship doesn't go over an hour. "I just think it's really important," she said, "to finish on time, especially for visitors." We were talking about worship. I was about to explain why it is hard to stay within an hour every Sunday when another woman in the conversation asked the key question: "Where does it say that we have to finish in an hour?" Then the picture came into focus. "Nowhere," added another, "it's just an expectation people have."

I liked the woman's question, and the other woman's response. Just where is it written that worship has to be done in an hour? *Nowhere* is, of course, the correct response. But it *is* an expectation many people bring to church. These same people will sit for hours watching television or a ball game, but let the worship service run fifteen minutes longer than they expect, and they become frustrated. Let it interfere with watching a ball game or getting to the restaurant before the Sunday crowd hits, and they become angry.

Ministers often joke about it, but in reality it's no laughing matter. The "one hour" attitude toward worship reveals an attitude about church we need to take seriously. It bespeaks a kind of "fast-food" mentality wherein people come to church to get a quick spiritual boost with no time wasted, in and out as soon as possible. They know what they want, and if they don't get it, they are out of there, complaining about the "service."

This way of thinking can be found among people who are quite committed to the church. The man who raises his arm and points to his watch supports his church with his presence and money. So too does the woman concerned about worship's being limited to an hour. The issue is not the person, but the way she or he understands the nature of the church. More to the point, it's about *the impact cultural values are having on the way church members themselves view the church.* We live in a fast-food, on-the-run society. People want what they want as fast as they can get it. If they don't get it immediately, they try somewhere else.

Here is the dilemma for churches today. Being influenced by the dominant culture is nothing new for American churches. The period of the great Western revivals was in response to the need to try to "win" members and financial support for churches independent of state support. But today we are in a time of numerical and financial decline wherein megachurches are booming and non-megachurches are struggling to survive. This makes leaders even more vulnerable to the pressure from a consumeristic churchgoing public to give them what they want. Of course, not everyone comes to church with this kind of attitude. All churches have faithful members who genuinely love and serve Jesus and make numerous sacrifices on behalf of their church. The point is, *these people are not the majority, and that is what creates the pressure.* Truth be told, this has always been the case. First Church, Main Street, USA, has been living by the 80/20 principle since it was founded. Eighty percent of the people who attend church watch twenty percent do all the work. This means most of the people who show up on Sunday do nothing but that.

Although this is the way it's always been, there is a difference now. Overall numbers are much smaller today, giving more power to the 80 percent who can and do vote with their feet and their pocketbook. Give them what they want or they will go or give somewhere else. Their power comes from the fact that most churches cannot afford to lose them, nominally involved as they may be. When churches were full, the nominally involved had little power to affect decisions about ministry. They could go somewhere else, and the average church didn't feel the impact. Usually someone else took their place the next week.

That's the way it used to work. For most churches, it is not that way anymore. Now they feel the impact of losing even one family. To a degree greater than ever before, ministers are feeling the pressure to give people what they want in order to have even a church half full of the nominally involved. What this points to is the real and dangerous crisis of integrity all of us concerned about the church are facing. The crisis is seen in the open and subtle ways in which churches and ministers now factor in the issue of attendance in the decisions they make. It is seen in the pressure lay leaders often put on clergy to increase membership. It is seen in the discouragement among laity and clergy when new things are tried with no measurable improvement in attendance.

Questions involving the integrity of ministry confront ministers and churches weekly because of declining attendance. New churches like Spirit of Joy don't just want people to attend. We *must* have new people to survive. We do not face the issue of decline. We face the real prospect of death. With denominational funding limited, time is not on our side. In a matter of less than five years we will know whether we will sink or swim in this sea called new church establishment. But at what price do we seek to grow numerically and financially? As we see visitors come and go, to what extent do we seek to meet all their needs and expectations in order to get them not only to come but to stay?

Denominational funding was essential for us even to begin. But that in itself adds to the pressure. It is no secret how mainline Protestant denominations define success these days. Publishing an annual book of statistics that is supposed to tell us how we are doing as the body of Christ leaves little doubt that the bottom line is about numbers, both money and people. After all, this is a financial investment the denomination is making. No one wants to put money into a failing venture. It is only natural, and even justified in some respects, to want a measurable return on the investment.

So the pressure to perform is real, whether it be a new church or an established one. As we have said, in many respects this has always been the case in the modern church. But the difference today is that numerical and financial decline have made churches much more vulnerable to the market-driven culture surrounding them. For the first time the prospect of extinction is real for denominations as well as congregations.

What is interesting is that this crisis of integrity in ministry is not confined to mainline churches. In a book titled *Can We Save the Evangelical Church?* Bill Hull, a pastor and former denominational executive in the Evangelical Free Church of America, argues that his church has lost its way.

> The problem of the evangelical church is multidimensional. Many churches are trapped in a bureaucratic morass. Our best people are involved in keeping the machinery moving, rather than out on the front lines where they belong. We spend most of our money on ourselves, making sure we are full-service, Christian outlets. Our pastors are frustrated, our lay people burned out, and our programs superficial.[16]

The book is organized around seven steps for renewal. A brief summary of each one will show that they speak as much to mainliners as to self-avowed evangelicals:

1. *We must heed the lion's roar.*
   Because renewal of the church begins in the heart of believers, they must want it before it will happen. Churches can no longer not know or not want to know they are in trouble. The prophetic call to listen afresh to the Lord's call (Am. 3:8) must be heeded. Hull cites sufficient statistical evidence that challenges unfounded assertions about church attendance and how many Americans pray daily.

2. *We must develop principle-based training.*
   Without effective leaders who are clear about the basic biblical principles of a mission-focused church, we are left with leadership spending all their time on the lookout for the latest model of "success" without concern for the spiritual foundations of such models.

3. *We must transform existing leadership.*
   Too many current leaders are entrenched and unwilling to change. Hull says they are not "spiritually motivated or ministry-minded." We need "metaleaders," he says, that is, leaders who have been transformed into principle-based leaders.

4. *We must cast the vision.*
   Ministers need to learn how to lead through the pulpit. It may be true that sermons alone cannot renew a church, but it is just as true that without preaching that inspires and teaches a compelling vision for the laity, there is no chance of renewal.

5. *We must sacrifice forms for function.*
   "Bureaucracy is eating the heart out of the evangelical church." Traditional structures too often stand in the way of mission. Hull believes in a "ministerial congregationalism" where daily decisions that don't alter the church's mission are left to ministers so that laypersons are free to do "people-focused" ministry.

6. *We must create community.*
Hull elaborates on the need for small groups that can nurture members in discipleship and disciple-making and get beyond what churches call fellowship, which "is nothing more than superficial 'pap.'" As he says, "Talking about the world and the weather around the coffeepot once a week does not qualify as koinonia."

7. *We must really do evangelism.*
Telling others about Christ. This, he says, is the responsibility of every church member. It's not happening, but it must if there is any hope of new life in the church, as well as the tell-tale sign of it.

These steps apply to any and all churches. We're all in the same boat whether we realize it or not. This news will not in itself change things for the better, but it does let us know that we are not alone in the problem we face. More important, though, is that the covenant membership approach deals directly with the situation. It provides an alternative that can make a significant impact on a church's life.

But let's be honest. A major obstacle to covenant membership is the 80 percent we mentioned earlier who actually attend weekly worship but do nothing else. They don't know there's a problem because they don't know enough about the gospel to know integrity is an issue. A few of them may spend personal time reading and studying scripture and enjoy a vibrant prayer life, but it is not a stretch to suppose that this is hardly true for most of them. They come to church and they go home. They probably try to live a decent life during the week. But any knowledge they have of the gospel is piecemeal, which often leads to wrong conclusions about what the gospel is really about and what being a church member really means. The notion that they spend any significant time in spiritual enrichment is at best a hope.

Of course, being in the 20 percent group is no guarantee that one's understanding of the gospel or the meaning of church membership is better than those in the 80 percent group, although their level of participation does give reason to think it is. But that is really not the main point either. The crucial thing is that the 80 percent *hold the power* to influence the church because the 20 percent are constantly trying to figure out ways to get the 80 percent more involved. In other words, the 80 percent group, by virtue of not being involved, are the consumers, and consumers hold the power in a market-driven culture. In a new church, power tilts even more to the 80 percent because numerical growth is not simply desirable but necessary. Indeed, the combination of a culturally conditioned view of success in the church and consumeristic thinking in the general public means we are in the ironic position of the unchurched holding all the power in a new church.

It is not difficult to see the pressure at work in this situation that leads ministers and churches to lower the threshold for membership as much as possible. The reality of what it takes to survive as an institution in a market-driven culture has put all churches in jeopardy. But the basic question is not one of survival. It is one of integrity. *What Christians today must face is the truth that the loss of integrity in ministry is a fate worse than institutional death.*

I do not write these words with ease or comfort. I write them as one whose financial future, and that of my mate in life and ministry, depends solely on the well-being of a new church whose institutional future is far from secure. But I also know Jesus calls all of us to obedience, not to success, and that it is possible to be successful institutionally while failing spiritually.

Recently Joy and I heard John Ortberg of Willow Creek Community Church talk about what it takes to follow Jesus.[17] His text was Peter trying to walk on the water to meet Jesus (Mt. 14:22-33), but sinking when he took his eyes off of Jesus and let his fears overcome him. He went on to say that whenever we take risks in ministry, it requires us to get out of the boat. Simultaneously we turned to each other and said, "We've gotten out of the boat."

That, however, wasn't the primary point of our identification with Peter. The thing that made us feel most vulnerable was knowing that we also face the danger of our fears overcoming us and making us sink. That is the reality with which we live day and night. We are out of the boat of security and into unsettled and uncertain waters. It is a choice we have made. But that doesn't make facing our fear of failing and all that would entail any easier. Yet we know that which Peter found out—that our hope is in Jesus. That sounds trite, but for us it is an existential reality. Sinking is well within the possibilities. Walking on the water is not, except that we keep our eyes on Jesus.

But the good news, the important news, is that knowing this is the case is the key to maintaining integrity in this ministry, or in any ministry. The only power ministers and churches have to resist the pressure of dancing to whatever tune it takes to get people to come to church or stay is knowing genuine survival in ministry is more about keeping our eyes on Jesus than sitting safely in the boat.

But there is yet another fact of life we have to understand if we are to cope with the crisis confronting us. It is the uncomfortable reality that *the institutional church is the boat!* The church of Jesus Christ itself needs to be evangelized. Even among the 20 percent who do more than attend on Sunday, there are those who refuse to step out of the boat, who resist making the decision to follow Jesus at all costs. Consequently, they make decisions that have the effect of making the church the boat we all need to get out of. They do this not because they are bad people. They are among the best the church has, in fact. They do it because they do not realize the current state of the church is like a body battling a serious internal infection that will require a new approach to stop its spread.

3

A Brief Excursus
How Things Got This Way

How did we get here? The history of church membership could provide an informative perspective on the subject. At the very least it could help us realize we didn't get to where we are overnight. The problem is, no such history exists. But there is a story, and telling it can give us a reasonable picture of the church's journey to its present land.

After the resurrection the disciples who had first followed Jesus came out of hiding and started preaching that God had raised him from the dead and made him Savior of the world. Their story was that God sent Jesus to die on the cross for sin, and all people had to do to be saved was to believe, repent, and be baptized. The response, as we would say today, was encouraging. But not everybody was happy about it.

One guy named Saul, a Pharisee from Tarsus, decided it was his duty to find these people and haul them into Jewish court for undermining the Jewish faith. His work was going well until he started out for the city of Damascus, where everything abruptly changed. He lost his eyesight for a time, and the story he told was that the Jesus whose followers he was arresting met him in a light so bright it blinded him, asked him what in the world he thought he was doing, then sent him into town to wait for further instructions. The experience was so compelling that Saul changed his name to Paul and joined up with the Christians. But not everybody was happy about it.

A lot of the Christians Saul was after thought his going blind was the punishment of God and that he was using it as a ploy to entrap them by pretending he was one of them. A Christian named Ananias had a vision in which he was told to go to this man and welcome him into the church as a brother in Christ. He didn't want to do it, and told God he didn't, but he went anyway. That changed everything. Paul started off preaching about Jesus in synagogues, but not many people listened. He decided to preach to non-Jews, and they did. It was amazing. So many listened that churches were started wherever he went. But not everybody was happy about it.

The Jews who had become Christians continued to keep Torah Law. They wanted all the Gentile Christians to do the same thing. Saul, who was now Paul, didn't agree. They had a big debate about it and Paul won the argument. That changed everything again, and not everybody was happy about that either.

Not many years passed before there were more Gentile Christians in the church than Jewish ones. By the first third of the second century, Judaism and Christianity went in different directions, with a lot of conflict before and after the fact. There are no records of how many Christians there were during this time. The physician/writer Luke tells us the church got started in a big way when three thousand were converted by the apostle Peter's preaching on Pentecost right after Jesus was crucified and raised to new life. While imprisoned on the Isle of Patmos at the beginning of the second century, a Christian named John said only 144,000 people would be saved at the end of time, which he thought was about to happen. That was probably as many Christians as John knew existed at the time, but we have no way of verifying that for sure.

What we have by the third century are small groups of Christians throughout the Holy Roman Empire who kept no records of how many of them there were. For good reason too. You could be killed for being a Christian. It wasn't something you wanted everybody to know about. Then the Emperor Constantine got converted in the fourth century. Once again everything changed. It became legal to be a Christian, so Christians started coming out of the woodwork, or catacombs, as the case may be. We don't know how many there were, but it's certain there were more than anybody had known about.

It is not until near the end of the fourth century that we get a good picture of how many church members there were in the Roman Empire. Everybody was. That's because the Emperor Theodosius I essentially made it illegal not to be, so people joined the church by the thousands. It didn't matter much whether they really believed in Jesus as God's Son or that he was raised from the dead. What mattered was being baptized, because it kept you alive. All this time there was only one church, which within a couple of centuries came to be known as the Roman Catholic Church because the bishop of Rome became the most powerful bishop in the civilized world. Thus, "Roman" because power was centered in Rome and "Catholic" because it was the one universal church. Soon the bishop of Rome began to be called the pope, "papas" or "father." He still is today.

By the year 1000 a centuries-old controversy and power struggle between the patriarchs (heads of the churches) of the Eastern Orthodox churches centered in Constantinople and the bishop of Rome produced a permanent split between the two centers of Christianity. We don't know how many members went with each group, but it was still the practice at that time for everyone to be baptized. It is not stretching the truth to say that as the population grew, so did church rolls. But we have no idea how many actual practicing Christians there were, even among priests and bishops, some of whom were in the church not so much to preach the gospel but to gain money, power, and influence.

By the sixteenth century corruption was commonplace, as the church lived off the backs of the peasants it ruled over with the help of provincial princes, who were beholden to the church for its blessings. In such circumstances there are always sincere people who finally reach their breaking point. A Catholic monk named Martin Luther was one of them. Upset about the church's blasphemous practice of selling indulgences to peasants in exchange for getting their loved ones out of purgatory, along with the general state of the church, Luther bravely posted his arguments for changing things on his church door in Wittenberg, Germany. Not everybody was happy about it.

It didn't matter. His defiance of church authority immediately erupted into what became the "peasants rebellion" that enveloped not only the church but the whole of Europe. These "protestants" (people who protest), as they were called, grew to such numbers that they formed a church of their own free from the power and dominance of the bishop of Rome. What was amazing is they made it stick. All the various Protestant churches of today throughout the world are the result.

King Henry VIII of England also got into the act of defying the bishop of Rome but for reasons very different from Luther's concerns. He wanted his marriage to Catherine of Aragon annulled so he could marry Anne Boleyn of France. The pope refused. In the ensuing crisis Henry named himself the supreme head of the Church of England, with the then archbishop of Canterbury, Thomas Cranmer, serving as his co-conspirator. The result was the permanent establishment of the Anglican Church, independent of all ties to Rome.

Yet the growth and development of European Protestantism did not necessarily change the lives of ordinary citizens for the better. When it came to power and greed and injustice, only the names changed. Not everybody was happy about it.

When the new world of North America was born, most settlers wanted no part of the church holding power over their lives as they had experienced in Europe. Protestant and Catholic churches in some colonies made attempts to duplicate their

European counterparts, but in the end the spirit of liberty prevailed not only in government, but also in religion. Citizens enjoyed freedom of and freedom from religion. This changed things even more.

Because the church became an arm of the Empire after Constantine, church membership in Europe could no longer be seen as a reliable sign of genuine Christian discipleship. The same held true in the nascent colonies of America, but for different reasons. Severed from the power of the state as its advocate and protector, and from the wealth of the Roman church, Protestant churches turned to persuasion for winning popular support. In the process they became voluntary organizations in which the wants and needs of members became paramount. Having submitted to the cultural ethic of individualism, churches turned their attention to growth in membership, without equal concern for discipline or accountability. As a result membership rolls grew, but without much concern that they reflect an accurate assessment of who was and was not truly Christian. As a result, church membership became as meaningless in gauging genuine commitment to the gospel of Christ in the new world as it was in Europe. And not everybody was happy about it! Some still aren't.

4

Church Shopping
Making a Bad Situation Worse

I had no more than introduced myself to the family attending our church for the first time when the wife said boldly, "We're church shopping." There was a declarative tone to her words, as if she wanted to ward off any possible misunderstanding about their motivation for coming. The unstated message of which she may or may not have been conscious was, "We are consumers, and we're checking you out to see how you compare with others." Quite often this is what we encounter at our church. On the surface, shopping for a church sounds like a reasonable thing to do that the current approach to membership takes for granted. After all, people have different needs and desires and not every church can satisfy them with equal effectiveness, especially those of children and youth. Studies tell us parents usually go where their children seem the happiest, so for them a large part of "church shopping" is looking out for their children's best interests. At the same time churches manifest varying degrees of spiritual aliveness. People are naturally attracted to those that seem more alive than others. Nothing wrong with that, of course, or in general the desire to seek a church in which one feels comfortable, except that it may reflect an attitude about church membership that runs counter to scripture.

In Romans 12:2 the apostle Paul writes, "Do not be conformed to this world, but be transformed by the renewing of your minds, so that you may discern what is the will of God— what is good and acceptable and perfect." In short, the church must not let itself be "fashioned to the age," much the way a potter shapes a piece of clay. It must not let the values of the dominant culture influence it in such a way that it compromises the demands of the gospel.

It doesn't take many conversations with visitors to our church to realize that their "shopping" attitude is an example of the extent to which they are "fashioned to the age" in the way they think about church membership. They are manifesting a "me-ism" way of thinking that dominates American culture. It's all about what I want, what I'm looking for, what I can get. This is the way we think as consumers. Shopping is for our benefit. It's about our getting the best bargain, finding what we want for the cheapest price. While this is the nature of shopping, there was a time when it was different because of the loyalty that existed between sellers and buyers. That was when people were customers rather than consumers and store owners were persons with names like Mr. Teague and Dr. Massey instead of corporations called Kroger's or Wal-Mart. Merchants actually thought about the interests of their customers back then, and customers were willing to pay a little more because of the personal relationship they enjoyed with the store owner or store workers.

Today it's about getting the best deal. So it is only natural for people to think about finding a church the same way, though they may not put it in those terms. In the next chapter we will discuss the biblical basis for covenant membership. For now we can say that the trouble with "church shopping" is that it shows how little people actually know about the nature of membership in the body of Christ. It encourages the thinking covenant membership challenges, which says that belonging to the church is about getting rather than giving, about getting the best deal rather than being called into servanthood. It overshadows or ignores completely the fact that church membership is about being a disciple of Jesus Christ's, about belonging to his body called the church, and can never be primarily about finding the services we want from an organization that goes by the name "church." A "church shopping" attitude tends to make people immune to the real reason for joining a church simply by virtue of the superficial commitment it tends to foster. There are, of course, exceptions to this rule, but they are the exception and not the rule, and that is the problem.

The covenant membership approach makes a subtle but significant difference in the way people approach finding a church. It becomes a matter for prayer rather than shopping, looking for signs that indicate the specific community of faith Jesus is calling us to be part of. When church membership is seen as a privilege, the choice of where to plant one's feet naturally becomes an opportunity to seek to please God rather than one's self.

Of course, our personal reaction to a particular church is important. Our needs do matter and so do the quality and focus of a church's ministry. We can trust God to work through our thoughts and feelings in leading us to a church. But it's all about "listening" for the decision instead of making one, of honestly seeking to sense the Spirit's leading in finding a church home, even as we did when we confessed Jesus and were baptized into the church. That decision, and all decisions related to church membership, involve a lot more than simply what we like and don't like.

The gospel stands in complete contradistinction to "me-ism." Jesus said it as plainly as it can be stated: "If any want to become my followers, let them deny themselves and take up their cross and follow me" (Mk. 8:34). Whether or not we believe these words of Jesus will be revealed in how we think about the way we should go about finding a church. If it is about us only, then it is obvious that we do not believe Jesus is serious about self-denial's being a prerequisite for discipleship.

But in many respects *it is the practice of churches trying to appeal to people who come with a church shopper mentality that is the real problem.* They may think they are trying to reach the unchurched by "meeting them where they are," but that doesn't stand up under scrutiny. For one thing, many church shoppers are people already "churched" who are looking because they have moved or have become dissatisfied in a previous church. A more accurate description of these people is "church switchers," not unchurched.

When it comes to the genuinely unchurched, the challenge is not to be all we can be to them. It is to have the integrity to be all we are to Jesus Christ without apology and trust the Holy Spirit to use that witness to disturb them out of their "me-ism," which is preventing them from taking the gospel seriously. This is why the logic of "seeker-friendly" worship services where a congregation falls all over itself not to be "too religious" or "offensive" continues to escape me. Having contemporary worship that is exciting and appealing to people outside the church is a bogus issue. What Christian doesn't need that? The real issue is the church's ability to remain clear about who is the subject and who is the object of our worship. This is what covenant membership does. It challenges the whole business of "seeker worship," which smacks of solipsism that is bound to offend the Lord it is intended to serve. As one colleague put it, "Seeker friendly services focus on the pew instead of the altar."

His statement is very clarifying. "Seeker-friendly" worship services are simply another way churches are being "consumer friendly." Once that line is crossed, integrity is hard pressed to have a voice in decisions made, because we are confused not only about worship but also about what it means to belong to the church. Granted the church may have turned people off. Granted the church may itself stand in the way of the gospel's being effectively proclaimed. What that means is the church stands in need of repentance, in need of getting its mind off itself and "stayed on Jesus," in need of transformation. But none of that is accomplished by developing a "consumer-friendly" approach to ministry that allows people who don't have a clue about the gospel to shape the church's life and ministry. That is equivalent to trying to solve an internal problem externally. It may be an acceptable thing—even desirable—to be "consumer friendly" at the door when the people we call "seekers" show up, but they will only add to the problem unless they are met at the altar with a standard of membership that makes joining the church mean something.

Mainline churches and mainline ministers tend to think they are not party to the desire to be consumer friendly. It is common to hear them criticize megachurches as "entertainment centers" trying to draw the biggest crowd. But this is little more than seeing the speck in another person's eye while missing the plank in one's own. Mainline "consumer friendliness" takes the form of excessive accommodation to religious pluralism that undercuts the distinctiveness of the Christian gospel. The valuing of religious tolerance has led to the devaluing of Christian particularity. Let me cite a case in point.

A visiting professor at the seminary where I used to teach took his turn in leading the weekly Communion service. It is a short service consisting of a couple of hymns, a prayer, and a homily focused on the meaning of the table. The professor stood in front of the table set with the emblems of Christ's body and blood and stated boldly that everyone was invited, Christian or not. The church, he said, had no right to exclude anyone. Several "amens" could be heard in the congregation. For this man, and those who agreed with him, concern for religious tolerance among Christians had reached such a high pitch that it superseded the fact that the table he spoke of was the table of Jesus Christ, a table with unambiguous particularity, a table around which the church as the body of Christ gathers to experience the living presence of its Lord. It was an example of an otherwise appropriate concern gone awry.

The problem of excessive individualism is also complicated by intolerance among mainliners for communal authority of any kind. The Church of the Savior in Washington, D.C., is a well-known community of faith that not only defines very specifically the terms of membership, but holds members accountable to them through the use of written spiritual reports within their mission groups. In numerous church settings and seminary classes I have shared their experience. Without exception it has been viewed as unacceptable authoritarianism that excludes people from the church. When pressed about the matter of membership accountability, the response is consistently that it is an individual decision.

A case in point. Once members of a United Methodist Church, a family I know stopped attending for a variety of reasons. Soon thereafter they received a call from the church asking for a financial pledge to support next year's budget. The husband refused, telling the caller the family was currently looking for another church. He was offended when the person then asked if they would consider taking their names off the church roll. In a subsequent conversation I told him I agreed with the caller. The family's name on the roll meant the church would have to pay conference dues on them. Because he was candid with the caller about their desire to find another church, the man was simply taking him at his word. But in my friend's mind removing his name from the roll should have been his decision alone. What he didn't realize was just how American his attitude about church membership was.

It is curious that people view membership standards as an infringement on individualism, and thus intolerant or exclusive, without seeing the similarity between commitment standards in the church and similar ways other organizations they belong to engage in this practice. PTAs have membership dues, civic clubs have attendance policies, community literacy agencies require training for tutors. It's all the same practice, but people think about religion in such individualistic terms that they consider it an unacceptable practice for the church to make them accountable for membership commitment. In general most people are more American than biblical in the way they understand the church and what it means to belong to it. The individual makes the decision, without much thought about any role the community of faith might have in the process, something we shall discuss in detail in the next chapter. In this kind of environment it is only natural that shopping for a church is done in the same way one shops for anything else.

But do we actually believe this is what Jesus has in mind when he calls people to follow him? Do we even believe he does the calling? If we do, then how can we justify his church's making membership an easy step requiring only a minimal degree of thought, prayer, and discernment? These questions inevitably come to mind when church membership is viewed from a biblical perspective, and it is to this topic that we now turn our attention.

5

Biblical Reflections

Testing Membership "Spirits"

The German word *Zeitgeist* means "the spirit of the time." I believe it is an appropriate term for the current state of church membership. It has become a reflection of the times in which we are living. At the same time, it is not a new situation. Since the fourth century church membership has been defined more by the culture than by its biblical roots. For this reason the scriptural admonishment to first-century Christians to distinguish the voices of truth from the voices of false teaching speaks to twenty-first century Christians as well: "Beloved, do not believe every spirit, but test the spirits to see whether they are from God; for many false prophets have gone out into the world" (1 Jn. 4:1).

Covenant membership is not simply an idea. It is an effort to take scripture seriously within the realities of institutional church life as we know it. One way it does this, as we noted earlier when discussing church shopping, is to approach membership from the perspective that it is the culmination of discerning the Spirit leading one into a particular community of faith. In Acts 2:47 we read the words "And day by day the Lord added to their number those who were being saved." In 1 Corinthians 12:18 Paul describes the church as the body of Christ, concluding, "But as it is, God arranged the members in the body, each one of them, as he chose." He reiterates this same point again in verse 24, "But God has so arranged the body, giving the greater honor to the inferior member."

All these texts naturally lead to the conclusion that joining a church is actually a response to a holy calling, and, thus, discernment, far more than "shopping around," aptly describes the way one should approach it. Time spent in prayer is more likely to lead to the right decision than comparing one church with another. Church membership is no willy-nilly process. It is an extension of the work of God begun in Jesus Christ to which the church is to witness. "Evangelism," says Will Willimon, "begins in the heart of God."[18] Church membership, therefore, when one truly commits one's self to being in the body of Christ, is a response to a divine initiative. It is not simply a matter of finding a place we like, but sensing we are being drawn into a community of people who were first claimed by God in and through Jesus Christ.

One might argue that expecting the unchurched to pray about finding a church is unrealistic. As a lay reader (see chapter 12) said of covenant membership:

> Thing is, this is an "inside" thing. This kind of commitment is almost meaningless to those on the outside. It would be irrelevant and probably a turn-off because it is so foreign, and I don't think it's our first priority to make people feel obligated to that. For those living in that corporate America, it will be miracle enough if someone wanders in and sings a praise song, and then wants to come back because they want to sing another.

I suspect the observation is correct, but it actually confirms the need for covenant membership rather than negating it. The fact that people visit a church with little awareness of what being a member actually means is precisely the reason covenant membership is so needed. The same need also exists for most "switchers." Covenant membership meets them where they are and invites them, not into membership, but to "live" with a community of faith long enough to learn how it understands and lives out the claims of the gospel *before* joining. In this way covenant membership trusts the Holy Spirit to nudge people into decisions as they stay with a community for a while. For numerically declining churches, and even new church starts, this may appear to be taking the risk of losing potential members. But covenant membership takes the opposite view. It says the real risk is allowing people to join when they do not know what they are doing and/or are not ready to make a genuine commitment to being a member.

Admittedly this is not an easy road to travel, because there are risks. There is the risk of being considered exclusive or judgmental about who is a Christian and who is not. But scripture provides us with no process for determining what it means to belong to the church except that the church does it on the basis of its discernment of New Testament standards. As a part of this struggle for integrity, churches will have to learn how to let people go, even as Jesus let the young ruler who would not give up possessions standing between him and Jesus walk away.

Is this easy to do? Absolutely not. One Sunday a family of four (parents and two elementary aged children) attended worship. We were immediately drawn to them. It was a Sunday when everything seemed to go right in the service, which in a new church is more the exception than the rule. Afterward they stayed and visited during fellowship hour. But it was a summer Sunday early in our life as a congregation, and in this area attendance in the summer sees more of a "drop" than a "slump." This couple obviously felt the effects of our being small. It was a dead giveaway, in fact, when they both commented, "But you're so small." We never saw them again.

What we have learned is what is really quite obvious. It takes special people to want to become a part of a new church early in its life. God has sent us some, and some have come on their own. The latter ones have never stayed around. Is that a rationalization for losing people? We don't think so. We've asked people why they have chosen to stay. No single answer has emerged, but what they all have in common is a sense that God led them to Spirit of Joy. This doesn't mean the people who chose not to come back weren't seeking the leading of the Spirit in their decision about a church. In some instances that is a fair conclusion based on conversation with them. But some of them were being led to other churches, and for that we can rejoice.

One of the ways we have sought to emphasize this point to the congregation is our adoption of the Quaker practice of "holding people in the light." Sometimes when we pray for others we are not always sure what to ask for from God. *Holding people in the light* means bringing them prayerfully before God and supporting them in this way. This allows us to leave to God what God wants to do for the person while becoming more open ourselves to trusting the wisdom and guidance of the Holy Spirit. Today we practice this form of praying for every visitor to our church.

That God calls people into churches reflects the very nature of God's relationship to the community of faith as a whole. The Bible speaks of it as a "covenant." God made a covenant with Abraham, with Moses, and through Jesus with the church. The word means "pact" or "agreement." In the biblical context, however, it is no ordinary agreement. The kind of covenant God makes is like that which exists between a king and his vassals. It is a pact not between equals, but one in which one serves the other. Yet both parties agree to be faithful to the covenant obligations. Christians can be confident of God's faithfulness. In turn, God expects faithfulness from us. Through Jesus, the seed of Abraham, we have become members of the covenant people (Gal. 3:6–9). He is the way God made us heirs to the promise of blessing God made to Abraham (Gen. 12:3). Thus, being a member of the church means living in covenant relationship with Jesus. Paul calls it being Christ's body (1 Cor.

12). It is more than believing in Jesus. It is living with him as the resurrected Lord of the church. There is only one head of the church, and that is Jesus Christ. He is the one to whom all of us are ultimately accountable as members of his church.

From this perspective it is easy to see that the church's mission is actually a simple one—to teach the gospel to those who know nothing about it with the expectation that the Holy Spirit will use this mission to convert people's loyalty away from themselves and to Jesus as God's life-giver. Church members are we who have responded to this nudging of the Holy Spirit, confessed our sins, and been baptized into the community of faith that bears the name of Jesus. We do not live with any illusion about how short we fall in attaining the goal of loving and serving Jesus. Being in the church is a practical way of keeping us on the journey and strengthening our resolve to put God before anyone and anything else (Mt. 6:33). The Christian way may not be easy, but the purpose of our lives is unambiguous.

Because of what we believe and have experienced, Christians view people of no faith as those who have not responded to the Holy Spirit. They live with ambivalence about what really matters in life because they are caught in the dilemma of trying to serve multiple loyalties. Following and serving Jesus settles that issue for Christians. There is one loyalty above all others, and that one loyalty is determinative in the value we place on all others. This is what being a member of the church means. It is a public statement of the priorities in life we are seeking to follow. Being together with other Christians connects us to the source of power to make this happen. That is why church membership stands over against the radical individualism of the dominant culture. It is a decision to be in community with others who are struggling to live the same way.

Everything the church does should nurture members in their desire to remain faithful to the one true loyalty that defines Christian living. This means worship, study, prayer, retreats, and ministry are the focal point in church life because they serve this purpose. The church's mission in the world cannot be fulfilled without members' being inwardly prepared to witness through word and deed to the life-giving experience they are having with Jesus. In other words, the church gathers to serve the church scattered. By having specific expectations, covenant membership commits the church to living up to this responsibility in clear and succinct ways. Indeed, the explicit nature of our covenant pledge takes literally the conviction that beyond preparation for discipleship everything else the church does falls into the "all other things" category.

But here is the rub. It is a widely held belief that nobody has time to live this way, except clergy, priests, and nuns, and they are paid to do it. At least, as we have noted, that's what many people think. Ordinary people have to make a living, support a family, pay the bills, spend time with the kids, volunteer in the P.T.A., Girl Scouts, or Lion's club, as well as find some down time to relax. Securing the future as best they can and taking every precaution against possible emergencies seems to be the only sensible way to live. Church is fine as long as it doesn't take too much time. That's the bottom line, but it of course extends beyond the issue of time to the question of commitment. For most of the 80 percent (who attend only), and even some of the 20 percent (who do all the work), commitment to the church is one among many in their lives, and even then it is barely holding its own.

Covenant membership says the opposite. It asserts that life in the church is not seasonal, nor is it secondary to everything else that might be put on the schedule. Not to participate in weekly worship, study, retreats, and ministry, and supporting all that with daily prayer, is the same thing as being a non-functioning organ of the human body. That is how important church members are to one another and to Jesus, who is the head of the body.

There is scriptural basis for this. A man comes up to Jesus and says he wants to follow him, but first he needs to go bury his father, who just died. Nobody in today's church, including the pastor, would argue with him. But Jesus said no, that's not how it works. Following me comes first (Mt. 8:21–22). Are we to suppose that we have become more sensitive to people's needs today than Jesus was? Or is it that Jesus was teaching the man that following him means nothing—absolutely nothing—if anything can take precedence over that relationship? How easy it is for family and work and even friends to crowd our lives to the point where all the church can hope for is "leftover" time. It's the way it is, but it is clearly not the way it is supposed to be.

The argument, of course, is that being a good parent and working hard to provide for our children is serving Jesus. That can be the case, but only if these loyalties do not become substitutes for nurturing our relationship with Jesus. What lesson are children of church members learning when their parents allow them to participate in athletics during times of worship? What is the message when soccer or ice hockey practice means missing corporate worship? Once in a church we served we had a couple who were absent from Palm Sunday worship because their son had a soccer game. They regretted it, they said, but "what can we do?"

I suspect, were he alive today, Olympic sprinter Eric Liddell would have an answer to the question. Liddell was the son of a Scottish family that spent their lives as missionaries in China. He was also a member of the British track and field team that competed in the 1924 Summer Olympics held in Paris. The film *Chariots of Fire* chronicled the story of this amazing group of athletes, considered the best British Olympic team ever. Liddell and his teammate and rival sprinter Harold Abrahams led a remarkable triumph over the favored American athletes.

It almost didn't happen, though. Not only did God make Eric Liddell fast, he made him a courageous Christian. Liddell had beaten Abrahams in the 100 meter dash prior to the Paris games. All of England and Scotland were sure he would bring home the gold. But as the team boarded ship to set sail for France, Liddell was told the qualifying races for the 100 were scheduled for Sunday. He refused to run, and a crisis ensued. He had regrets about his decision, he would later say, but no doubts. It was the

Sabbath, and that was all he needed to know to make his decision. Great pressure was applied to change his mind. Even the then Prince of Wales appealed to his sense of patriotism. But Liddell refused to go against his own conscience.

Abrahams ended up winning the gold. But the story does not end there. Liddell's teammate, Lord Andrew Lindsay, having already won a medal in the hurdles and aware of the conflict between Liddell and the British Olympic Committee, made the magnanimous gesture of requesting Liddell be allowed to run the 400 meter dash in his place. They agreed, and Liddell won the race, completing a triumph for the British team never equaled before or since.

One view of Liddell's refusal to run the race he had trained for three years to win is that he was being too legalistic in his attitude. But that would miss the point, wouldn't it? The story is about commitment, about sacrificing for one's convictions, about putting God before personal gain or glory. Children today are being taught by their churchgoing parents that worship is secondary to their desire to play a game, whereas a generation ago the fastest sprinter in the world gave up a sure gold medal because he believed just the opposite. This is the place we have reached in church life. It would be surprising if the church's children today had even the faintest understanding of why he did such a thing.

The point is not that parents should make children sacrifice for the beliefs of their parents. That would do little more than drive them away by pitting the church against their desire to play sports or something else, especially when the need to fit in is so strong. The issue is what is being taught and whether or not any serious attempt is being made to model for children the priority church life holds in the lives of its members. It is not hard to imagine how this could be done. A simple discussion with children as they begin participating in sports and other activities about the church's place in family life would be a good beginning. It is not all that difficult to establish the fact that there is no rule that declares sports must have priority over church. There is also the option of attending worship at an alternate time than Sunday, even if in another church, as a way of underscoring the importance of worship, not to mention the sacrifice the rest of the family is making for one of its own.

The goal is to ensure our children know missing worship is a serious issue, rather than shrugging our shoulders with a sigh and a "What can we do?" In reality, parents make children do many things they believe are important even when the children don't. School is one example. Music lessons are another. Even participating in a sport fits this category. Why is it that church members think church is not worthy of the same type of parental guidance? The answer, of course, is that membership has become so casual it just doesn't seem all that important to miss a Sunday or two or three or a month of Sundays.

Yet it is unmistakably clear in the texts we have reviewed that Jesus leaves no room for hedging. Everything in the life of a Christian, including family, and certainly work and recreation, can become idolatrous if we are not careful. One of the values of church membership is to remind us of this important truth. But too often churches themselves never raise the issue out of fear they will lose families if they do.

That might in fact be the case. But the reality is that losing a person who is half-hearted in commitment to the church is only to confirm what has already taken place in the person's heart. *Nominal church membership is membership in an organization, but it falls short of being membership in the body of Christ.* Worse, though, is the fact that the traditional approach, which counts the nominally committed as members, may contribute to their failure in understanding the difference. Further, as we have shown, the evidence is overwhelming that once in this state, they seldom move to deeper commitment. Once on the fringes, they stay on the fringes. Churches may get their money, but they don't get the person.

The issue is quite simple: Covenant membership declares that membership and discipleship are indistinguishable. Being a church member means being a functioning part of the body of Christ. In the first and second centuries the fact that membership put believers in personal jeopardy didn't leave much room for half-hearted commitment. What the first church members knew is that faith and obedience go together. It means nothing to say that one believes in Jesus but chooses not to be obedient in following him. Jesus himself said this: "Not everyone who says to me, 'Lord, Lord,' will enter the kingdom of heaven, but only the one who does the will of my Father in heaven" (Mt. 7:21). And this: "Enter through the narrow gate; for the gate is wide and the road is easy that leads to destruction, and there are many who take it. For the gate is narrow and the road is hard that leads to life, and there are few who find it" (Mt. 7:13–14). Do we believe what Jesus says? This is a question churches must answer when they think about how to do membership. The danger of cheap grace Bonhoeffer warned us about remains:

> Cheap grace is the preaching of forgiveness without requiring repentance, baptism without church discipline, Communion without confession, absolution without personal confession. Cheap grace is grace without discipleship, grave without the cross, grace without Jesus Christ, living and incarnate.[19]

When one reads such a statement as this or takes the words of Jesus seriously, it is an enigma why churches continue to think they can let people join at the lowest common denominator of commitment and expect them to become more committed later. It is as if the modern church has decided it has wisdom about human nature that Jesus did not have.

One of the frustrating realities about traditional membership is that today's clergy find themselves spending more and more time attending to the wants and needs of members. It's called maintenance ministry and is the inevitable result of the influence of a consumer mentality on the church. Consumers, whether in the marketplace or in the church, want their needs met. As the saying goes, they can always take their "business" somewhere else. There are, of course, many church members who do not think this way, but the consumer mindset is nonetheless a fact in church life today that makes it harder and harder for churches to be the church.

If, then, spiritual stagnation accounts for the anemic condition of so many churches today, as I have argued elsewhere, the easy path to membership is the most obvious practical expression of it. It is also the most obvious thing churches can do something about. We cannot force people to take faith seriously, but the church can say that it is no longer willing to accommodate people who do not have an earnest desire to love and serve Jesus Christ. Things can in fact be different in the church. We can change the way people think about membership. We can begin limiting the influence of the dominant culture on the church's life and witness as churches confess they have made the gate wide and the road as easy as possible for people to join, and become willing to end the practice of perpetuating membership rolls that do not reflect the ranks of genuine discipleship. How to do that is the question to which we now turn our attention.

6

Holding Up Progress

Personal Obstacles to Covenant Membership

The word *obstacle* means "something that stands in the way of or holds up progress toward a goal." There are two types of obstacles standing in the way of churches moving to covenant membership. One is personal, the other institutional. This chapter addresses the former; the latter is addressed in the chapter that follows.

Covenant membership is a concept that will stretch mainline church members to rethink their understanding of church life. As a rule, spiritual disciplines are not something they practice with any regularity or even associate with membership in the church. For the sincerely committed, joining the church is still a matter of putting one's name on the roll and trying to live the best life one can. This approach is so deeply ingrained that resistance to covenant membership will be almost immediate. But experience has shown that awareness of the specific nature of this resistance helps people cope with it.

On a personal level, resistance arises from several factors. One is doubt. Interestingly enough, the word *doubt* means "deep thought." Perhaps this is why many Christian thinkers have considered doubt in positive rather than negative ways. Even the Christian writer Oswald Chambers commented, "Doubt is not always a sign that a man is wrong; it may be a sign that he is thinking." Tillich said doubt was not the opposite of faith, but an element of it. Bacon went so far as to declare, "If a man begins with certainties, he shall end in doubts; but if he begins with doubts, he shall end in certainties." Perhaps skeptic Betrand Russell put it best when he advised, "It's a healthy thing now and then to hang a question mark on the things you have long taken for granted." What person who thinks deeply doesn't have questions about God, especially in the face of unmerited suffering around the world? What person who thinks deeply does not wonder about the validity of the church when the atrocities committed by the church in the name of Christ through the centuries are honestly faced? Tillich was right. Doubt is an element of faith, at least of intelligent faith.

From this perspective, doubt does not necessarily have to be a negative force working against covenant making. Covenant membership invites people from the sidelines or from being spectators into full participation in the life of the church. Such a specific challenge can tap into doubts a person might have because it requires a decision to be made. The call to commitment can raise the issue of doubt. This can be a healthy thing so long as it doesn't become a shield for avoiding making a choice to commit one's self fully to being a member of the body of Christ.

Because it is an element of faith, Jesus meets us in our doubts. At least, this is how we can read his encounter with the one who is called "doubting Thomas," the one who perhaps more than the other disciples is a mirror into which we modern Christians can look to see ourselves. The story in John's gospel (20:19–29) says the raised Jesus revealed himself to the disciples while they were gathered in secret in the home of one of the members of the group. When they told Thomas, who had not been with them, what had happened, he scoffed at their words. He had to see for himself, even touch the nail prints, to believe such a thing had occurred. Later, the story says, Jesus appeared again and met Thomas at the point of his doubts, to which this doubting one responded, "My Lord, and my God." Jesus commended those who believed but had not seen, but at no point did he chastise Thomas for his doubting.

The issue is whether or not we use our doubts to come to faith and strengthen our commitment to Christ and his church, or whether we swim in a sea of questions as a way to avoid making the choice. Covenant membership does not require one to have no doubts, or to avoid troubling questions. Just the opposite. It is an invitation to become a member of the community of faith within which doubts can be confronted. Not only did Jesus not reject Thomas because of his doubts, but also neither did the other disciples. That is the power of covenant community.

Lukewarmness is a second obstacle to covenant membership and one of the most difficult to do anything about (see Rev. 3:14–22). Essentially it is the absence of any hunger or thirst for righteousness (Mt. 5:6), faith without passion, conviction without courage. It neither takes faith seriously nor questions its validity. Lukewarm involvement in the church has no spiritual depth and engages in nothing that might be legitimately called faith formation. It's like cotton candy, with an appearance of substance but vacuous when bitten into. Lukewarm church members are usually polite and pleasant, interested in what is going on, but only from a distance. They see themselves as staying above the politics of church life, which creates tension and controversy. They might lend a helping hand once in a while as long as there is no serious or long-term commitment involved.

It is an obstacle fraught with danger because it is so respectable, so nice, so easy. But it destroys any chance for genuine discipleship. Matters such as justice and integrity or threats to human existence are viewed as beyond one's control. Take life as it comes and don't get upset about things. Roll with the punches. To a lukewarm church member, Bonhoeffer's claim that when Jesus calls us to discipleship, he is bidding us to come and die[20] sounds like the exaggerated imagining of someone who has gotten carried away by it all.

If covenant membership helps at all in overcoming this obstacle, it is by holding out the hope that by practicing the spiritual discipline of membership one will be confronted by the risen Lord in a fresh and energizing way. Bonhoeffer said that obedience creates the environment where faith becomes possible.[21] By being a practical way to test the truth of this claim, covenant membership can disrupt lukewarmness enough to make serious commitment possible. But the obedience has to come first.

Another obstacle is the practical reality of busyness. Although busyness is not a new problem, we often think it is. It's as if no generation has ever faced the press of schedules we face. But Jesus' parable of the great banquet (Lk. 14:15–24) suggests just the opposite. Someone gives a great banquet and sends out his servant with personal invitations to guests. This is how the text says they responded:

> But they all alike began to make excuses. The first said to him, "I have bought a piece of land, and I must go out and see it; please accept my regrets." Another said, "I have bought five yoke of oxen, and I am going to try them out; please accept my regrets." Another said, "I have just been married, and therefore I cannot come." So the slave returned and reported this to his master. (14:18–21)

The man's response was not one of understanding. He saw the excuses for what they were. He sent the servants back out to find any who would come to enjoy the feast, and declared that "none of those who were invited will taste my dinner" (14:24).

The parable is, of course, a picture of the messianic banquet at the end of the ages, but it holds implications for life now as well. Is it too much to think that life in the church can be like a great banquet? Not when one participates at a deep level in koinonia, in community in Christ. Trust in the power of koinonia is foundational for covenant membership, the trust that making this kind of commitment brings blessings to overflowing. A major weakness of traditional church membership is that it opens the door for members to miss the great banquet by institutionalizing swimming in shallow waters. Excuses for nominal involvement have no consequences. Covenant membership, on the other hand, enables churches to confront busyness as an excuse for messed up priorities and confused values. In this way covenant membership presses church members to choose between commitment and spectatorship. This is not a negative action on the part of the church, for it is in knowing where we stand that we can see the choices clearly and also their consequences. Obstacles to commitment can never be overcome so long as they are not seen for what they are.

A fourth obstacle is fear of not living up to covenant expectations. It is a fear that may be rooted in a sense of personal inadequacy, an awareness of the very thing the apostle Paul confessed: "I do not understand my own actions. For I do not do what I want, but I do the very thing I hate" (Rom. 7:15); or the truth of the words, "It is a fearful thing to fall into the hands of the living God" (Heb. 10:31). Instead of responding in faith, some people allow fear to become an obstacle to commitment. It grips them, and they cannot move. A loathing of hypocrisy in others may be part of it as well. They have seen too many church members who do not take commitment seriously. They do not want to be among them. What they do not see, though, is that taking covenant as seriously as they do is good reason to enter into it.

The truth, though, is that this is an unnecessary obstacle to covenant membership. Clergy, for example, are the first to admit to a strong sense of inadequacy and a fear of not being able to live up to the expectations of the church when they answered the call to ministry. I used to tell students who felt this way that they just might make fine ministers. I would have been more concerned had they expressed confidence in their worthiness.

The truth of the gospel is that it is a fearful thing to fall into the hands of the living God.

The strength of covenant membership is that it yokes people together to share the burden of the journey, and that gives us strength we do not otherwise have. No one measures up perfectly to covenant expectations, but when left to struggle alone, one is likely to quit the journey. Coupled together, people help each other along the way, something one of the wisdom writers understood clearly: "Two are better than one, because they have a good reward for their toil. For if they fall, one will lift up the other; but woe to one who is alone and falls and does not have another to help" (Eccl. 4:9–10). Then we learn the liberating truth that, as Brendan Francis once observed, "our fears are tissue-paper thin, and a single courageous step would carry us clear through them."[22]

A fifth obstacle is mistaking talent for spiritual giftedness. People who do not have obvious talents in music, art, speaking in public, leading a group, organizing a task, or in the ways they see others exhibiting talent feel they have nothing to contribute to a group's life. Therefore, finding a ministry to which they can give themselves is more difficult. The problem is that they do not understand the difference between human talents and spiritual gifts, mainly because churches have not taught them the distinction. A human talent can be developed and refined, but a spiritual gift comes from one's relationship to Jesus. It is something other than and more than a talent. It is an expression of grace and love Jesus gives to a group through its members. It is an expression of the presence of Christ, which means a sign of a spiritual gift is when a group grows toward spiritual maturity. This is the whole purpose of spiritual gifts:

> But each of us was given grace according to the measure of Christ's gift…The gifts he gave were that some would be apostles, some prophets, some evangelists, some pastors and teachers, to equip the saints for the work of ministry, for building up the body of Christ, until all of

us come to the unity of the faith and of the knowledge
of the Son of God, to maturity, to the measure of the
full stature of Christ. (Eph. 4:7, 11–13)

One of the problems with traditional church membership
is that it settles for talents rather than evoking spiritual gifts.
Through involvement in ministry groups, churches practicing
covenant membership have a means of focusing on members
discovering their spiritual gifts. Once they claim their gift they
can have clarity about the specific ministry in which they want
to be involved. The difficulty is getting people to take the risk
of becoming a covenant member to experience the truth that
they have a spiritual gift. But at least covenant membership can
fulfill its promise to them if given the chance.

One other obstacle to mention is one's unwillingness to be
stretched in uncomfortable ways. The church has members who
do not want to be disturbed by controversial issues, complicated
decisions, or prophetic challenges to rethink their personal value
system and lifestyle. This is not what they give their money for.
They want to be with people they enjoy being around and to
help out in little ways to keep the organization running smoothly.
The promise of being stretched out of their comfort zone will
probably not appeal to them.

The nature of spiritual growth is, of course, to stretch us in
precisely this way, which is why we chose to say it in our covenant
pledge at Spirit of Joy. It is unavoidable when dealing with God.
Wilderness travel is part of the journey. Making decisions while
trusting the leading Spirit of the One who cannot be seen rather
than having all the loose ends tied up, what the apostle Paul
called walking by faith and not by sight (2 Cor. 5:7), is part of
the journey. Getting out of the boat to meet Jesus on uncertain
waters is part of the journey. Letting go and falling into the
grace of God is part of the journey. It's all about being stretched
in uncomfortable ways, this thing called Christian discipleship.
Covenant membership helps with this in the same way it does
in overcoming some of the other obstacles. It puts us in the

company of people on the same journey with the same struggles. No one has a map to easy spiritual growth. But traveling together certainly makes the journey easier. Covenant membership can at least offer a hand to hold on to and a point of reference that reminds them of the commitment they have made to the community.

There are other personal obstacles to covenant membership, but all of them reveal the same basic need—a willingness to relinquish one's autonomy to the will of Jesus Christ and his body, the church. The problem, of course, is that we live in a society that encourages acquisition. Accumulating is the name of the consumer game all of us play, even if we call ourselves Christian. Giving up anything is about as un-American as one can imagine. We don't give up. We take. We possess. We hold on to, whether it be money, power, position, or control. The call to relinquishment, then, strikes us as from another world, a world of the first century when life was simpler and God could be taken more seriously. The world today is anything but simple, making it necessary to allegorize the teachings of Jesus, if not acknowledge they were meant for a world that no longer exists.

In one form or another this is the way Americans think, and churches have been slow coming to grips with it. We have wanted to believe that the call to discipleship was compatible with the values of American culture. Naïve about the negative side of capitalism, we have ignored the power of consumerism to undercut Christian discipleship. Instead, we have "domesticated" the gospel to make it fit the American context. One of the manifestations of this is the fact that "in practice, Christian communities have failed to build few bridges between the task of ecclesiastical funding and striving to live 'stewardly' lives. We can talk the talk, but how do we walk the walk? How do we get from money to lifestyle in a truly meaningful way?"[23]

These questions go to the heart of what it means to live as Christians amid the affluence we enjoy. Churches have done little to help members find a way. Although several reasons lie behind this value, an important one is the way we do membership. The power of covenant membership is that it offers a way to help people build a bridge between giving money to support the church and living *stewardly* lives. In short, covenant membership takes relinquishment seriously. It seeks to embody the truth that it is in giving our lives for the sake of the gospel that we find them, that in giving up and giving in to the reign of God we gain. The very nature of covenant is that it costs us something. We get into the banquet free because of divine grace, but we don't get away before it has cost us everything. We discover no sacrifice compares to the richness of being the friend of Jesus (Jn. 15:14).

7

Privatized Religion

The Enemy of Covenant Community

Covenant membership is a practical approach to help churches to become the community in Christ they are called to be. Privatized religion is its enemy because it promotes the notion that faith is nobody's business but one's own, that a relationship with God is only and solely between the individual and God. We have already noted the fact that radical individualism has had a significant influence on the way American Christians think about their relationship to God and their relationship to the church. In this sense they are more "American" than "Christian," though for most church members the two are indistinguishable.

That is part of the problem. They don't realize just how American they are as Christians, going back to the founding of the nation. It was the eighteenth-century philosopher John Locke who argued persuasively for the primacy of the individual over society. The drive for freedom and independence and the challenge of conquering an open frontier made Americans predictably receptive to his thinking. Radical individualism was the result. It was inevitable that the Christian gospel, what with its own emphasis on freedom from the law and its message of individual justification and salvation, would be heard by the inhabitants of the new world as consistent with Lockean philosophy.

This union produced a church membership with the philosophy of autonomy of the individual deeply rooted in its worldview. It may come as small comfort to know that the church is not alone in its struggle against excessive individualism. A recent study found that the synagogue is facing the same pressure. Unlike their parents and grandparents, young Jews are "more willing to say for themselves what it means to be Jewish, more focused on an interior spiritual life rather than deferring to age-old custom to define them as Jewish."[24] The study goes on to say that this development "poses challenges for a minority seeking to maintain its identity in the face of pressures to conform to the dominant culture."[25]

Yet the New Testament unequivocally emphasizes community in its effort to balance the personal and the communal. For covenant membership to find any receptivity among mainline churches we must understand that radical individualism is anathema to the gospel of Jesus Christ. At the very least, we can say that Jesus envisioned a community living under his Lordship, not an organization living by Robert's Rules of Order. He spoke to followers, not to a follower, to those who would become the community we know as the church, as the body of Christ. Just as individuals need a family within which to grow up into emotionally healthy adults, so Christians need the family called the church to grow up into spiritually healthy adults. Jesus would be shocked, if not appalled, by the privatized faith of so many American Christians today. He was a Jew, and what mattered to Jews—then and now—was community. The fate of any individual was inextricably bound to the fate of the community. Covenant membership is an attempt to reclaim this dimension of our heritage, to embody the conviction that the gospel calls us to a life of faith that is both personal and community based.

One serious effect of this loss of awareness of the relationship between the individual and the community has been the misguided notion among Christians that they can take or leave the church, but in either instance the church is optional. No surprise, then, that the idea of the church holding members accountable for their membership covenant would meet with immediate resistance. "What right does the church have to say anything about my relationship to God?" is a common response to this concept. "I try to be a Christian, so what right does the church have telling me I have to do these other things to belong?" is another one. What church members who hold this view do not realize is how American they are in their sentiments and how far removed they are from New Testament Christianity.

But radical individualism not only distorts the relationship between the Christian and the church; it also pits the two against each other. "For the common good" is considered a justification for the hegemony of the status quo, or for church authority. This creates an environment of suspicion that works against the mutual support among members that community makes possible. It also casts responsibility to others in a negative light, making genuine commitment to the whole less likely. *Authority* and *authoritarian* become synonymous.

This is the state of the church in America today, which is why the concept of covenant membership goes against the grain of most mainline churches. Steeped in a liberalism that thrives on individualism, we have shaped our life together in such a way as not to infringe upon personal liberty or sovereignty. Yet often we are unconscious of how deeply ingrained individualism is in us. Therefore, rather than viewing accountability as a practical means of helping people fulfill their responsibilities to the group, we see it as an effort to control or impose views on them.

The church, of course, is not blameless in this situation. It has misused and abused its authority more than once and has sometimes been paranoid about individuals and groups it has perceived as threats to its power or influence. It has sometimes tried to use its authority to promote a moralistic understanding of the gospel that reflected immaturity rather than wisdom. A neighbor recently told me that his church did this by saying that those who smoked or drank alcohol were disqualified as candidates for deacon. Some churches focus on obvious behaviors they consider wrong, such as drinking or smoking or sexual immorality, in an effort to hold members or leaders accountable while ignoring the "weightier matters of the law" such as issues of racial, social, or economic justice. As a result, most have now thrown the proverbial baby out with the bath water. The problem is not the church's effort to have members make good on promises made but the standards being used to define what that means. The lack of integrity and emphasis on trivialities always undercut respect for authority. But this should not serve as a justification for churches' rejecting the very thing that can make them stronger. Covenant membership can flourish in congregations that are conscious of the power of their collective life in helping individual members grow and mature in their faith.

The word *community* is overused, but it does reflect the New Testament perspective on church life. The word most often associated with "community" is the New Testament term *koinonia,* but it is actually the word for "fellowship." In Acts 2:42 we read, "They devoted themselves to the apostles' teaching and fellowship, to the breaking of bread and the prayers." The early Christians spent time listening to the instructions of the apostles and sharing the common bond of fellowship they had with one another through Jesus. It doesn't take a lot of thought to understand that this was not a community without accountability or expectations. The "instructions of the apostles" means the teachings of those who had been with Jesus, that is, the Twelve (minus Judas, replaced by Matthias). The Didache, as their teachings were called, and which is extant, consisted of the apostles' understanding of the teachings of Jesus and what they believed were the essential elements for life together in the church. These instructions were not subject to debate or alteration. They were the rule of order for the early church.

There was also the breaking of bread, literally a meal that ended with the Lord's supper, and prayers. Koinonia— fellowship—was the byproduct of the presence of Jesus among them both in the apostles' teachings and the breaking of bread. This was life in the early church. Simple and straightforward. New Christians had to be taught the meaning of Jesus' life, death, and resurrection, which formed the basis of Christian identity. They were instructed in the teachings of Jesus in order to know how to live the new life they had experienced through faith in him. The first Christians did whatever it took to strengthen one another in both Christian identity and Christian lifestyle. This was their first and only concern. It would have no doubt sounded strange to them, if not heretical, to hear modern Christians speak of individual autonomy. To enter Christian fellowship meant just the opposite—giving up one's autonomy to belong to Christ and become a member of the church. They would have recognized immediately that insistence on one's independence from the whole would have disastrous consequences on their nascent community. It would mean missing the opportunity to learn the story of God's salvation in Jesus from those who had been with him, struggling to live as a follower of Jesus without the guidance and support of the community, and thus weakening their witness to Jesus, and would have made unity of spirit and purpose impossible.

We can learn from their example, which is what covenant membership seeks to do. It is not autocratic or authoritarian. It is both communal and representative. Thus, it challenges the widespread sentiment that the good of the whole is important only if it does not impinge on individual freedom. Covenant membership acknowledges the personal dimension of faith while promoting responsibility and accountability to the whole. In this way each member plays a role in holding the community accountable for faithfulness and justice seeking. It is the way for the church to be the church, which is the primary way it nurtures faith in and witness to its Lord.

8

Adaptation

Stability in a Sea of Change

The adoption of covenant membership will certainly involve a significant change in the way churches approach joining the church. We all know that change is not a word that gets much welcome in most churches. Yet it is obviously the only way anything can be different. The reality is that change comes to every group whether the members welcome it or not. But learning to adjust to it is the key to using change to accomplish the group's purpose more effectively.

The Latin root of the word *adapt* means "to fit to." It points to an ability to adjust to changing conditions, a quality necessary not simply for survival, but for *effectiveness*. Living where I do, every year I have the opportunity to see this at work in a dramatic fashion. Snow is a part of life in Minnesota. But it seems that being able to drive in it is a learned skill easily forgotten. So when the first snowfall comes, cars are all over the roads. Weather reporters urge people to adapt: "It's wintertime again, folks. Drive like it." Once they do, life goes on without much delay or serious problems. But it takes some adaptation before that happens.

This is the way life is because change is the rule. The issue really is not "change." That would be like saying the issue is weather. We will never do anything about the weather except to adapt to whatever conditions we face. That's the way life is. It seems, though, that many people view change as a matter of "appeasement," of making compromises that compel us to give up what we really believe or believe in. But that is not what is involved. *Change is about adaptation, the ability to fit ourselves to the circumstances precisely for the purpose of maintaining stability.* Ironically, for this reason adaptation is in fact the way the church preserves that which is essential for its identity and mission. Resistance to adaptation makes the church vulnerable to the power of social change just as an oak tree is more vulnerable to a storm than a palm tree. Adaptation is the means by which the church uses the inevitability of change to serve its purposes rather than be adversely affected by it.

The church of the twenty-first century can no longer afford to play games with itself or with its Lord. Adaptation isn't a choice. It's a necessity. We continue to talk as if the church still had the option of going in the direction it has been going. It does not. Institutionalism has led the church into serious compromise of its integrity. Compare today's churches with the growth of Alcoholics Anonymous, the cornerstone group for all other twelve-step groups. AA groups do not maintain a membership roll, in most cases own no property, keep administrative costs to a minimum, and exist solely and completely for the mission for which they came into existence—to help people stay sober. That mission is the determinative force in all decisions. Under no circumstances are the demands of the twelve steps ever minimized just to get someone to attend a meeting.

This is a picture of the church as it is supposed to be. But it is not how we function, and there is a reason. The weight of institutionalism has pushed the church's mission to the periphery. If AA functioned as most churches do, members would find little help in getting sober, but they would probably have a very nice place to gather. Obviously the church cannot reinvent itself, although that prospect has much for which to commend itself. The church is not going to shed its excessive institutional needs and turn itself into small groups spread across the land that actually help people to depend on God in order to get through the day. But the church could reorganize itself so that its mission of teaching the gospel to all peoples becomes its primary concern. But that means changing. Given the state of things, the choice not to seems as foolish as driving into oncoming traffic on a crowded freeway.

One of the meanings of the word *change* is "to become deeper in tone." That is what we mean when we say the church needs to adapt. It needs to become deeper in tone, to be about essentials rather than peripherals, about substance rather than appearance, about significance rather than success. Attachment to externals stands in the way of going deeper, whether it be the beauty of a sanctuary, the location of a building, the prayer book used, the hymns sung, or the length of the worship service. None of these things truly matter to God. They can aid us in praising God, but to God they matter little. WE are what counts to God. Jesus Christ did not die on the cross for the beauty of a sanctuary, the location of a building, the prayer book we use, the hymns we sing, or how long the worship service lasts. New life for us is what the gospel is about, and that is what the church should be about. If truth be told, Jesus probably looks at twelve-step groups and says to himself, "That's what I had in mind!" Conversely, it is not a stretch to imagine he looks at churches and wonders how we got so far off the track.

It is an ironic twist of history that the very existence of the Bible, which is so often used to justify the status quo, is itself a product of adaptation by the believing communities that produced it. Even more so, the survival of Israel depended on its ancient story being adaptable to changing circumstances. In other words, the plaintive question of the psalmist, "How can we sing the Lord's song in a foreign land?" (137:4) was answered. The people found a way, which formed the basis for the emergence of Judaism out of the ashes of the Jerusalem temple when the exiles returned from Babylon. The Bible itself reflects this capacity to adapt in order to provide stability for the believing community. Thus writes James A. Sanders:

> The primary characteristic of canon, therefore, is its adaptability. Israel's canon was basically a story adaptable to a number of differing literary forms, adaptable to the varying fortunes of the people who found their identity in it, adaptable to widely scattered communities themselves adjusting to new or strange idioms of existence but retaining transnational identity, and adaptable to a sedentary or migratory life.[26]

It would seem only sensible that modern Christians learn the importance of adaptability from the sacred story from which we get our identity and understand how to live our faith in our own time. The church of America is in a land as foreign to the ways of the gospel as Babylon was to Torah. For churches to continue going in the direction they are going will never get them to where they want to be. The future is frightening only when we travel down the wrong road with no sense of who we are or what to do next. Covenant membership offers a change of direction. It is adaptation that offers a tangible way for the treasure to be preserved. Covenant membership is adaptation to a culture that no longer supports serious commitment to the church by creating a community that knows who it is and what it is to do to show it. Refusing to adapt denies the reality of the dominant culture and increases the potential for churches to lose their sense of identity and sight of their mission. A new direction is not only needed, it is a necessity if we are to sing the Lord's song in this foreign land.

Part of the reason resistance continues is because it is quite literally "built into" the institutional church. That is to say, the church is so big and clumsy that turning it around is, as a friend reminds me, similar to turning around an aircraft carrier. If it turns too fast the planes will fall off. Not really, but his point is well made. But that is hardly the problem these days. Worrying about churches turning around too fast would be a welcome problem. But the real problem is not turning at all.

Sometimes it helps to laugh at ourselves. I do that when I think about the classic comedy *Trains, Planes and Automobiles* in which John Candy and Steve Martin play two men who become an unlikely duo, thrown together by circumstances as each is attempting to get home for Thanksgiving. At one point they rent a car. John Candy volunteers to drive and takes the wheel, only to get on the freeway going in the wrong direction. A passenger in a car traveling parallel to them motions frantically. Candy waves, then realizes the man is yelling something. When he rolls down the window he hears him screaming, "You're going the wrong way!" to which he responds, "How does he know we're going the wrong way?" Minutes later, of course, they discover the truth for themselves, but by then it's too late. They barely escape with their lives.

Churches can be like John Candy driving the wrong way headlong into traffic while ignoring the warning call that they are going the wrong way. Covenant membership is an effort to roll down the window and yell, "You're going the wrong way" to mainline congregations. But they will not hear the call unless they are willing to deal constructively with change. That means the ministers of these congregations will have to help them. In some instances, however, they are the ones who are the most resistant to change. Consider the reflections below of a former student.

Our Charge Conference is coming up. Ugh. In Methodism, the Charge Conference is the way the local congregation stays connected with the larger church. At our Charge Conference, the District Superintendent attends and leads us as a representative of the Bishop. We make our reports about our work, we approve budget items for the coming year, we certify laity for offices in the church and elect them to those office[s].

The Charge Conference has been a part of Methodism for as long as there has been Methodism. As Methodism has become more and more entrenched in being an institution, the Charge Conference has become more and more burdened with administrative matters. What began several hundred years ago as a quarterly meeting to affirm the work of the church and celebrate God's work in the church through worship and communion has become near the end of this century a simple business meeting where the church presents its annual reports and statistics.

In the state where I minister our bishop made a bold move a few years back. He gave instructions through the District Superintendents that Charge Conferences were to become worship services again, and not just business meetings. You'd have thought he'd committed heresy, the way some folks complained.

Having been in the corporate world before I became a pastor, I thought it was a great move. Churches are not corporations—they don't need an annual stockholder report, or an annual session presided over by all of the chief officers of the organization. Churches need worship, celebration, a place for vision and passion and commitment. Now, we still do our business during that service of worship—we just do it within the context of a worship service and not as though it were a dry and boring meeting of executives.[27]

There is hope for the church when a United Methodist bishop changes the nature of a Charge Conference to ensure the church's business is grounded in its worship life. There is also hope for the church when a young United Methodist minister understands the church well enough to recognize the wisdom of the bishop's decision. But this hope runs headlong into the reality that the clergy criticized the bishop's decision. How odd it is when the Lord of the church says,

No one sews a piece of unshrunk cloth on an old cloak, for the patch pulls away from the cloak, and a worse tear is made. Neither is new wine put into old wineskins; otherwise, the skins burst, and the wine is spilled, and the skins are destroyed; but new wine is put into fresh wineskins, and so both are preserved. (Mt. 9:16–17)

If we believe Jesus, then refusing to adapt puts the church at risk of tearing at the very fabric of its existence. It is a common response to changing conditions. People respond in such a way that they put at risk the very thing they want to protect. Thirty years ago Alvin Toffler sought to alert us to this danger in his book *Future Shock*.[28] He provided a stunning analysis of the effect change was having on people then. All these years later his book offers important counsel to the church, not about change, but about adapting to it.

His thesis was quite simple. It is not the fact of change that throws people off balance. It is *the accelerated rate of change overwhelming our capacity to adapt* that is the problem. He called this condition "future shock." It happens, he says, when tomorrow impinges on today at such a rapid rate that we lose our balance. Put simply, "future shock is the human response to overstimulation."[29] The reaction encompasses the mental, psychological, emotional, and even physical dimensions of human life. Toffler argues that people must develop the capacity to adapt to a degree greater than they have previously *and* for society itself to recognize the reality of adaptive limitations so that the rate of change might be slowed to a reasonable pace. But, he says, it is folly to think that change can be stopped. *The real hope lies in adaptation.*

But, of course, that is impossible apart from the will to do it. Here Toffler is blunt in his assessment:

The disturbing fact is that the vast majority of people, including educated and otherwise sophisticated people, find the idea of change so threatening that they attempt to deny its existence. Even people who understand intellectually that change is accelerating have not yet internalized that knowledge, do not take this critical fact into account in planning their own personal lives.[30]

Concerned about the influence of bureaucrats who refuse to understand what is going on, Toffler is even more blunt:

> If failure to grasp this fact impairs one's ability to understand the present, it also leads otherwise intelligent men into total stupidity when they talk about the future. It encourages them to think in simple-minded straight lines...And it encourages us to worry about precisely the wrong things.[31]

That, in a nutshell, is precisely what is going on in churches. We are worrying about the wrong things. Here's the real deal: Churches need to stop worrying about their survival and get concerned about living and witnessing to the gospel. We act as if the only problem we have is overcoming the fact that people are not attending. In many ways that would make the challenge one of packaging the message in a more appealing way. But the more basic problem for the church is the fact that people are rejecting the gospel. This is not a problem a new package will solve. Learning how to preach and teach with integrity is what is needed. It begins with the church getting refocused on its identity and mission and becoming less concerned about maintaining itself. This is the intention and effect of covenant membership.

Resistance to adaptation leaves us with no alternative but to maintain the status quo. In reality it is a choice between new vitality and a continued spiritual decline, and perhaps even literal life and death for many congregations. Who among us believes Jesus wants his church to refuse to adapt to changing conditions? He is the one who came preaching change in Judaism, challenging the status quo because the religious leaders of his day were playing the game of keeping the cup clean on the outside while it was dirty on the inside (Mt. 23:25). To maintain the status quo means believing the church perfectly embodies the gospel and doesn't need reform or renewal. Only those who suffer from severe self-delusion can believe that. On the contrary, the church is called to adapt to changing conditions precisely because it is an earthen vessel for the gospel (2 Cor. 4:7), and the gospel outstrips our capacity to live faithfully.

The matter needs to be stated candidly: *Refusal to adapt is a sign of weak faith, and weak faith always produces unfaithfulness.* It represents an unwillingness to trust ourselves to Jesus. Faith is an act of the will. It is a choice to be made. Weak faith is a sign of a weak will, a fear of making the tough choice to throw in with the One who calls us to walk with him, even if it means on water. In Toffler's language, refusal to adapt means we are suffering from "future shock." The signs of this condition are easy to read.[32]

An obvious one is *outright denial.* Toffler says the denier's strategy is to "block out" unwelcome reality. It is a refusal to assimilate new information, which then makes possible the conclusion that "things really are the same, and that all evidences of change are merely superficial." I once knew a woman who embodied this attitude. A kind and loving person who never missed a Sunday at church, Alice was convinced the government had pulled a hoax on the American public in the summer of 1969 when it claimed to have landed a man on the moon. It was all filmed in California, she said. Not a word of it was true. There was no convincing her otherwise. The future had come too close for her comfort and shocked her senses to the point where her only means of coping was denial.

Key phrases that alert us to denial are "the more things change, the more they stay the same" or "there's nothing new under the sun." The struggle for churches is that deniers have to admit their problem before they can learn to adapt to change, and many of them are in positions to influence church decisions.

A second sign of future shock is *specialism.* "The Specialist doesn't block out *all* novel ideas or information," says Toffler. "Instead, he energetically attempts to keep pace with change— but only in a specific narrow sector of life." So the doctor who uses the latest technology to examine a patient will resist new music in the church service in the name of preserving the great hymns of the church, or an elementary school principal who is responsible for the education of the next generation of leaders wants them to dress the way he does when they pass the offering plates in church.

A third sign is *obsessive reversion* to previously successful adaptive routines that no longer work. We see this in the people who long for the good old days and in the people who gaze at crystals, both escaping from the world as it is into a world they imagine was or is real. We see it in the attitude that the poor are people who don't want to work and in the attitude that welfare reform is a conspiracy of the wealthy against the poor. In the church we see it in the romanticizing of the past as if the future of the church depends on going backward.

A fourth sign of future shock is *super-simplifying*. This is a response in which a future shock victim tries to cope through the illusion of simple answers. A perfect example of this response to the rapidity of change is the 1998 Kentucky law that extended the law permitting people to carry a concealed weapon (the "gunslinger's law") except in public institutions to allow clergy to carry a pistol when at church. The minister who proposed it claimed that the world as it is makes it no longer safe for him to carry church collections to his home or to the bank (one would hope the latter). He was convinced that carrying a concealed weapon at church would make him safe. The Kentucky legislature agreed. Super-simplifiers need to believe simple solutions will actually solve real problems. More police will reduce crime, just saying no will decrease drug abuse, eliminating questions about evolution on state competency tests will make it untrue, and on it goes. In the church we see this kind of response to change on a regular basis—ministers promote a new program to jump start their churches, laity search for a young minister who will attract youth, denominations launch capital programs to generate interest or start new churches as a way to secure the future. The seduction of super-simplifying is that it carries an element of truth in it, though ultimately it shows itself to be a half-truth that makes matters worse. The reason is easy enough to see. Life is not clear-cut or simple. It consists more of shades of gray than easily distinguishable colors. Simple solutions are simple, but never real solutions.

The problem, of course, is that people suffering from any or all of these symptoms of future shock don't recognize they are, and often when confronted will not admit it. Worse, many times they are quite persuasive in their arguments against change. Unfortunately, it only takes a few people to block adaptation. But the opposite is also true. It only takes a few courageous ones to begin the process. And in the church, hope springs eternal, because the resurrection assures us that when it comes to the things of God, the last word is always life, not death. Bodies can be transformed and people can adapt to changing circumstances.

Covenant membership does invite churches to change. It is, in truth, a call for churches "to become deeper in tone." And the stakes are high because the integrity of church membership is hanging very much in the balance today. Reformation is an urgent need. We can adapt and influence our own destiny or let social change sweep us aside. As Toffler puts it, "We have it in our power to shape change. We may choose one future over another. We cannot, however, maintain the past."[33]

9

Traveling Light

Proper "Dress" for a Covenant People

The Gothic cathedral of Chartres, France, is known for its majestic spires and beautiful stained-glass windows. Although perhaps the grandest of all cathedrals, it is but one of hundreds dotting the landscape of Europe. As such, they stand as symbols of the power and presence of Christianity in the world, not only in the past, but even today. In appearance alone they tell a story of the evolution of the church from a small band of disciples in the first century to a rich and powerful institution that wields influence and power throughout the world.

But is it possible this is a picture of a church traveling the wrong road rather than one that effectively witnesses to the Christian gospel? The Catholic, Orthodox, and Protestant churches today hold property and investments literally worth billions of dollars. Juxtapose this with the Lord of the church describing himself as not having anywhere to lay his head: "And Jesus said to him, 'Foxes have holes, and birds of the air have nests; but the Son of Man has nowhere to lay his head'" (Mt. 8:20).

Further, consider the fact that he sent out the Twelve on a mission with instructions to take very few material goods with them:

> Then Jesus called the twelve together and gave them power and authority over all demons and to cure diseases, and he sent them out to proclaim the kingdom of God and to heal. He said to them, "Take nothing for your journey, no staff, nor bag, nor bread, nor money—not even an extra tunic. Whatever house you enter, stay there, and leave from there. Wherever they do not welcome you, as you are leaving that town shake the dust off your feet as a testimony against them." They departed and went through the villages, bringing the good news and curing diseases everywhere. (Lk. 9:1–6)

"Take nothing for your journey." It would, of course, be naïve and counterproductive to call on churches today to give up owning property. But these words of Jesus at least challenge us to ask if the church has not come to the place where it is weighted down with "things" for the mission it has been called to fulfill. It is possible that the church has become like David equipped to do battle against Goliath wearing the heavy armor of Saul (1 Sam. 17:38–39) and is unable to witness with effectiveness.

The one thing we do know is that the church's mission is unambiguous. It is called to do spiritual battle with forces that would pretend to have the power of God. But contending with demons and sickness requires mobility, the capacity to move freely armed only with the power of God: "You come to me with sword and spear and javelin," David told Goliath, "but I come to you in the name of the LORD of hosts" (17:45). This is why the disciples are told to travel light as they are sent into the world to do battle with all spiritual powers and authorities that would claim the minds, hearts, and souls of women and men away from God. Their power is in the name of the Lord, not in the symbols of earthly dominion and authority.

The enemy with which they contended is, of course, still present. The powers of darkness that would seek to quench the light of God in Jesus are very real today. National Public Radio commentator Scott Simon reveals how real and powerful they are in his celebrated public television documentary *Affluenza*.[34] It is a real condition that is ubiquitous in our society today. Defined as "an unhappy condition of overload, debt, anxiety, and waste resulting from the dogged pursuit of more," the symptoms of affluenza are swollen expectations, hyper-commercialism, shopping fever, mounting bankruptcies, fractured families, chronic stress, social scars, and resource exhaustion. Between 1980 and 1995 expenditures for advertising aimed at making children consumers rose from $100 million to more than $1 billion. Companies are willing to pay $200,000 per commercial on Channel 1, the school news channel watched by millions of students every day. A popular game among children is "Mall Madness." The winner is the player who spends the most money and then gets to the parking lot first.

That is only the beginning. Researchers follow children around in stores and ask to see how their bedrooms are decorated in order to learn about their purchasing patterns. At a "Kids Conference" held at Disney World during the documentary, viewers listen in on a speaker who is addressing the need for ads directed at boys to be more aggressive to catch their attention. He actually makes the statement, "Antisocial behavior in pursuit of a product is a good thing." All this adds up to one thing, the film concludes: "Kids are a cash product to be harvested."

This is the spiritual battle churches are in the world to fight. But the question is, How well equipped are they for it? I believe the only honest answer is not well equipped at all, for the simple reason that the church looks more like the world than like the disciples Jesus originally sent into it. Sadly, the frequently made assessment that the world is in the church but the church is not in the world is true for too many congregations. A church doesn't have to be wealthy to be travelling with too much "stuff." Every conflict over accessories to the mission, whether it be insuring stained-glass windows, putting down new carpet, or renovating the pastor's study, is a sign of our problem. It's enough that these conflicts are common, but worse yet is the fact that few members pay attention to the real issue. They could do without the bickering, of course, but they fail to see the distance between the church and its Lord these possessions represent.

A minister was recently telling me that for months his church had been involved in a controversy over buying a grand piano for the sanctuary. Finally he persuaded a woman who wanted to give $25,000 to the church to earmark it for a piano. It wasn't the way he wanted her gift spent, but he saw no other way to move the governing board past this conflict over accessories for the journey. Upon announcing the gift in the meeting, he said the discussion immediately turned to using it as a basis for a campaign to raise sufficient funds to go the whole way and purchase a Steinway! This is a picture of the church of the Lord who had nowhere to lay his head.

The church's excess baggage is symptomatic of the real problem. That problem is the seduction of the church into trusting in the power of accessories for identity and security. But the lesson of scripture is clear. Power for the people of God has only one source. The story of Gideon is winsome in how it makes this point (Judg. 6—8).

Gideon was a judge in Israel of the tribe of Manasseh. But his family was the weakest clan in the tribe, and Gideon was the weakest member of his clan. Not much to build on here, yet the angel sent to tell him he would lead his tribe victoriously against the Midianites greeted him by saying, "The Lord is with you, you mighty warrior." Gideon protests, explaining his lowly state, but the angel will hear none of it. So Gideon asks for a sign that this is truly a message from God. He prepares a kid, unleavened cakes, and puts them in a basket, places it on a rock, and pours broth over all it. The angel touches it with his staff and everything vanishes in flames.

From here the story moves through several scenes where Gideon trusts God, then demands more signs in the well-known fleecing of the wool episode. Finally he sends out a call for help and 32,000 men respond. But God tells him he's got too many soldiers. Why? Because "Israel would only take the credit away from me, saying, 'My own hand has delivered me'" (7:2). Gideon is instructed to ask all who are afraid to go home. Twenty-two thousand men leave! But God is still not satisfied. Take the men down to the water, Gideon is told. Those who lap up water in their hands, as one would expect most of them to do, can go home. Those who lap like dogs can stay. Nine thousand, seven hundred are sent home, three hundred are left, and now God tells Gideon he is ready to do battle.

This is a story of utter dependence on God for survival. It is also the story of what churches have not listened to. In every way we can we have tried to secure ourselves for battle, but in the process we have become so encumbered by it all that we not only are ill equipped for the struggle, we are seldom in the struggle at all. Instead we are doing battle with one another over accessories that matter next to nothing to the Lord, who has nowhere to lay his head.

But what does this have to do with church membership? It has everything to do with membership because maintenance ministry requires a level of financial support that makes it the focus rather than the byproduct of commitment. The percentage game takes over. The coexistence of membership and discipleship becomes a way of life, a subtle but genuine accommodation to the values of the dominant culture, which are left unchallenged. Thus, the spiritual battle Jesus sends the church to wage is all but lost, which is why the "isms" that separate people in the larger culture are to be found in churches.

Still, one can hope for a realization that ministries of compassion can change this situation. "Communion with God, community with people, and compassion for the poor" is the way Henri Nouwen expressed it in the September 16 entry of a journal he kept in 1995 during a sabbatical year from Daybreak, the L'Arche community in Toronto where he served as pastor. The journal turned out to be the last book he would write. A year later he suffered a massive heart attack that took his life. In the entry he was describing the content of a mini-retreat he and his friend, Sue Moesteller, gave for guests at Daybreak. The call to covenant membership has a realistic chance in churches that understand and embrace the interrelatedness of these three dimensions.[35]

Mission and membership have for too long been thought of as categories distinct and distanced from each other, when in fact they are two sides of the same coin. The church's witness in the world cannot be separated from the members whose responsibility it is to carry it out. The integrity of the church's witness in the world depends on the integrity of its commitment to its mission to do battle with all the forces of society that would rob and imprison people. And the key to this commitment is the genuineness of one's membership in the church.

One of the curious things about the gospels is the almost casual way they speak of Jesus' compassion for the poor and the way the poor responded to him. In Luke we read about when some lepers approached Jesus for help as he was on the way to Jerusalem (17:11–19). Keeping the appropriate distance as the law required—the "unclean" did not comes close to the "clean" for fear of contamination—they hollered out for Jesus to have mercy on them. It was a remarkable thing for them to do. They risked rebuke, if not punishment, for such an act. Two blind men had once called out to Jesus for healing and for their trouble were "sternly" told by the crowds following him to shut up, but these two weren't easily deterred and shouted even louder (Mt. 20:29–31). Lepers were considered more dangerous than blind men, so ten was better than two. And as with the blind men, Jesus payed attention to their plea. He told them to go and show themselves to the priests as the law required. They left rejoicing at the new life they had been given, but one came back to thank him, and in doing so became the example for others to follow.

One wonders if these ten lepers got the courage to call out to Jesus because they had heard about the one Luke tells us about earlier in his gospel (5:12–14). It is a poignant story. The man comes to Jesus, prostrates himself at Jesus' feet, and begs, "Lord, if you choose, you can make me clean." Jesus' response is astounding. He touches the leper! And then Jesus says, "I do choose. Be made clean."

Those following Jesus may not have understood the breadth and depth of his compassion, but those who were its beneficiaries did. The benefit of the years separating us from the time of Jesus should lead churches to see the power of compassionate ministries. They are the tangible and embraceable means of experiencing the mighty power of God in the world today. When one considers the power of affluenza, for example, the battle in which we are engaged seems every bit as daunting as David facing Goliath. But this is precisely the situation that makes experiencing the power of God possible. The poor remind the church that it is supposed to be poor, not rich. They remind the church that it is supposed to be traveling light, not weighted down by accessories. They remind the church that it is to be doing battle for the minds, hearts, and souls of people against the principalities and powers of this age armed only with "the name of the Lord."

But only the committed among church members will be able to trust this message. That is also why the poor can save the church from itself. Members of an institution will likely trust only the resources of the institution's own making. It takes being a sincere member of the body of Christ to trust its Lord. Gideon could go to battle with three hundred men and David could face Goliath with a few stones only because they had faith in the power of God to protect them. The same is true for the church today. Why else would Jesus tell his disciples to go into the world taking nothing with them? They had to trust him, trust their faith in him, trust that he was with them all the time. This is the way the church is to live in the world.

In his book *Compassionate Ministry*, Bryan Stone concludes a discussion on the church's taking up the call to compassionate ministry with this challenge:

> The upshot of the foregoing is that the decision with which each of us is confronted by the God of Jesus is a faith decision—or, better, a decision to live by faith. But this decision is not some abstract acceptance or rejection of salvation understood as a private and interior experience or guarantee of heaven. This decision, because it is a decision to live, has content and meaning constituted by activity and commitment. The critical decision to which we are called by God in Jesus is fundamentally a decision to convert to compassion... It is a conversion to compassion as a way of life— a fundamental commitment to taking sides, being the neighbor, feeding the hungry, giving drink to the thirsty, inviting in the stranger, clothing the naked, visiting the sick and the imprisoned, setting the captive free, liberating the oppressed, and doing justice.[36]

This is a great challenge. But compassion always is. To rise to meet it means a change in attitude regarding the excess baggage most churches are carrying these days. Churches do not have to sell all their possessions to be faithful any more than rich people must give up all their wealth to be Christians. The core issue is *attachment*. It is the stickiness, if you will, of all the "stuff" churches own that undermines genuine commitment to Jesus. Breaking the bonds of attachment requires the conscious decision Stone calls the church to make. There is no hope apart from making this decision, but every hope of new life in churches if it is made.

But let us be clear about the practical meaning of this call for churches. The call is not to Christian activism, though being active is part of it. As Hauerwas and Willimon put it, "The church doesn't have a social strategy. The church *is* a social strategy."[37] The church is an alternative community to the idolatrous dominant culture in which it finds itself. Ministries of compassion are the church's light on the hill. They are the signs of who and whose we are.

To be this kind of church means having members who mean what they say when they confess Jesus as Savior and declare to live with him as Lord of their lives. The church as a community will live faithfully as the body of Christ only as its members practice their faith. Every faithful member cannot tolerate a church that looks more like the culture in which it exists than the demands of the gospel it proclaims. It is significant that the prophets of Israel linked unfaithfulness to God with trampling the poor. They saw Israel's idolatrous ways in selfishness and greed that led to ignoring those in greatest need.

> Thus says the LORD: For three transgressions of Israel, and for four, I will not revoke the punishment; because they sell the righteous for silver, and the needy for a pair of sandals—they who trample the head of the poor into the dust of the earth, and push the afflicted out of the way. (Am. 2:6–7)

So the plea was inevitable: "Let justice roll down like waters, and righteousness like an everflowing stream" (Am. 5:24). For the church of today, Amos's call to justice and righteousness means doing battle against the spiritual forces of darkness of the world that trampling on the poor represents.

There is no secret about why serious commitment is needed to remember the poor. Compassionate ministries are hard because the problems are so overwhelming and the issues run so deep. Such ministries are not for the fainthearted. Institutions collect food for the poor at Thanksgiving and Christmas. The poor are no doubt glad they do. When you are bleeding, having a Band-Aid is very important. But the body of Christ lives among the poor. The body of Christ wants to know them, love them, and bring them a word of hope. That takes time, energy, tenacity, commitment. No time for bickering about accessories. It will take all we have and more to stay with these ministries. But that is what it always takes to follow Jesus. That is why covenant membership and compassionate ministries depend one upon the other, one helping to make the other possible.

10

Educating Ministers

A Covenant Challenge to Seminaries

Covenant membership needs ministers who are strong in faith, deep in spirit, and unafraid to lead the church into change. It needs ministers who not only know scripture, but also believe without equivocation that Jesus is Savior and live in ways that show he is Lord of their lives. The reason churches need this kind of ministerial leadership is obvious. More than any other person, clergy influence the quality of life and witness in the churches they serve. But ministers cannot give what they do not possess, cannot lead if they do not know where to go, and cannot help others commit to something they themselves do not believe in.

Although many factors play a role in the church's having effective and committed leadership, none is more important than seminary education. Indeed, the quality of the church's ministerial leadership is in large measure determined by the quality of education seminaries provide. This being the case, it is also true that a major share of the responsibility for the state of mainline church life today rests with seminary education. I say this even as I have seen firsthand both as a student and a teacher the good work seminaries do. But in the overall scheme of things, they are not preparing ministers to be the leaders churches today need. As a teaching colleague used to say, "We are educating people for a church that doesn't exist." Another way of saying the same thing is that we are not educating people for the church that does exist.

No one is the culprit here. The problem is more subtle, a theological climate that is the result of the cumulative effect of a university model for educating ministers that does not fit the task or serve the needs of the church. As such, academic life is not a model for the kind of setting in which most clergy find themselves once they graduate. Yet teaching is a primary task ministers face. Covenant membership, for example, depends on ministers' educating church members about the nature of the church and its relationship to the dominant culture. So ministers are sent out to teach and preach in a setting that is not simply different from the academic life they have lived in for three or more years, but may even be hostile to the message they seek to bring. In these circumstances, knowledge and competency in skills are not enough to equip ministers for the challenges they face. The risks of trying to lead a church into a new way of thinking about ministry, and especially about membership, will be taken only by those whose have *a passion for the gospel.* This is the key to ministers' leading churches to a deeper level of commitment to discipleship and to the church's witness in the world.

To serve the church effectively the seminary environment needs to be shaped by the realization that knowledge and skills do not produce this kind of passion. They are, instead, servants of it. Passion for the gospel has but one source—a personal relationship with Jesus—and strengthening this relationship should be a primary concern of seminaries. This means seminaries need to be focused on students' spiritual formation as much as their intellectual development. The measure of their success should be the same as that of the church—helping people grow into faithful discipleship. The long-held notion that knowledge-based education is the business of seminaries, whereas formation is the business of the church, is a truncated view of theological education that has weakened church and seminary education alike. Churches need formation help from their seminaries in equipping clergy to lead churches to find their moorings in a society more likely to dismiss them than take them seriously.

But there is a formidable obstacle that prevents most seminaries from serving the church in this way. It is an *excessive relativism* that reveals the degree to which seminary education today has also accommodated itself to the dominant culture. The practical effect of excessive relativism is an easy tolerance for diversity and extremism, as if theological differences have no consequences. No one would accuse columnist Ellen Goodman of being conservative, but even she has recognized the limits of tolerance in the realm of ideas. Intrigued by the findings of a new poll that said the vast majority of Americans think evolution and creationism should co-exist in public schools, she decided to take a closer look. Sponsored by the liberal group People for the American Way, the survey, conducted by Daniel Yankelovich, was no multiple choice quick response poll, but an in-depth questionnaire of 1500 people. It found that 83 percent believe evolution should be taught in schools, which encouraged Goodman. But it also found that a nearly equal percentage thought creationism should also be taught, not as science but in some other area of the curriculum such as history or culture.

Ralph Neas of the sponsoring organization interpreted the results to mean "Most Americans believe that God created evolution." Perhaps, but Goodman dug a little deeper. She found that most of those surveyed couldn't fully define evolution or creationism, which led her to wonder: "So maybe they weren't wrestling with two incompatible views of human origins. Maybe it wasn't a struggle at all. Maybe it was: 'Creationism... evolution...whatever.'"

Disturbed by this possibility, she talked with theologian John Haught of Georgetown University and author of *God After*

Darwin. He compared the survey with what he sees in his classroom. "Today, there is more tolerance, but the passion for truth doesn't seem to be as strong as it could be." He continued, "There is less concern with getting to the 'True' with a capital T. You don't step on people's toes. You want to avoid conflict, including meaningful conflict." Goodman concludes that with all its strengths, liberal education has led to "a passive acceptance of all ideas as more or less equal," culminating in a loss of passion for truth and "a giant shrug of the shoulders" when confronting competing claims for truth.[38]

Henri Nouwen made a similar observation before his untimely death. Writing in his journal, which would chronicle the last year of his life, he reflected on the problem of sloth or laziness:

> The concept of sloth helps me to understand my own world a lot better. It is not evil or good but the passive indifference toward both that characterizes our attitudes. I can see how hard—yes, impossible—it is to preach to people who are slothful because nothing really matters to them. They don't get excited about a beautiful thought, a splendid idea, or an encouraging perspective, not do they become indignant about ugly words, sordid ideas, or destructive viewpoints. Evelyn Waugh, according to [Ralph C.] Wood, once called sloth the besetting later-modern sin. I believe Waugh is right. It seems the sin of a spoiled generation, for whom nothing really matters.[39]

This is the kind of environment in which mainline seminary students are being educated. It has created a kind of vacuous tolerance that leads vulnerable students to consider the Christian claim that Jesus Christ is essential to God's work of salvation as incompatible with the reality of today's religious pluralism. A case in point was the reception given to Maxie Dunnam, president of Asbury Theological Seminary in Kentucky, in a lecture during my teaching days. He argued for the need to make belief in Jesus Christ as the Son of God the center of Christian faith once again. Convinced the church was in a period of theological slippage, he suggested there were limits to tolerance and that the church should call anything that would undermine Jesus as the center of faith a heresy. At the same time he was equally emphatic in clarifying that his concern was heresy, not heretics. The distinction was completely lost on our students. More troubling, though, was their outright dismissal of his argument without any substantive engagement of his primary thesis.

The students' failure to see the need for passionate commitment to the gospel was a commentary on the negative effect excessive relativism is having on mainline seminary life. In some respects it is the inevitable byproduct of an uncritical acceptance of Enlightenment Christianity that puts more confidence in human progress than in the reality of God's daily guidance. Students graduate believing in relativism more than truth and in tolerance more than conviction. They have fallen into an intellectual malaise that refuses to proclaim the gospel of Christ as truth, as if doing so is tantamount to becoming a Christian zealot. They have failed to learn, or to be taught, that truth is not simply what one desires it to be and boldness of faith is not intolerance of the beliefs of others. They were schooled in a thorough knowledge of Bible, history, theology, and psychology, but received little help or even encouragement in knowing and loving the One whom they have been educated to serve. As a result, passion for the gospel has all but disappeared as a desirable quality in ministry.

Ironically, it is excessive relativism that ends up betraying the intellectual integrity it supposedly promotes. In the article noted earlier, Ellen Goodman mused that "sometimes an open mind comes perilously close to being an empty mind."[40] It is ironic that more than a few mainline clergy have crossed this line in the name of religious tolerance. More accurate is that it reveals shallow spiritual maturity. The danger, of course, is that ministers who do not know how to pray, or do not believe that prayer is anything central to their leadership in the church, cannot lead the church into renewal. Nor will the anemic spiritual state of mainline Protestantism be overcome by clergy who are not all that sure Jesus is the way, the truth, and the life, or that they can tell the truth they have found in him without claiming to know all truth there is.

At the same time there are pockets of encouragement on the seminary landscape. Some schools have taken steps to make formation a central part of their course of study. One example is Luther Seminary in St. Paul, Minnesota. Listed in the core curriculum for the master of divinity and master of arts degrees are three courses titled "The Call to Discipleship," "Discipleship I," and "Discipleship II." The first is "an introduction to what it means to be a follower of Jesus, through large group biblical presentations, worship, and reading and discussion on the Bible. Students and faculty together explore the meaning of discipleship in the Bible and for people of the Word today." The other two consist of group sessions with an advisor that include prayer, worship, and discussions about faith in daily life based on selected biblical texts. Although these are non-credit courses, they are required of all students in these programs. What is especially noteworthy is the fact that they are spread out over both the first and second years of study.

This is the kind of formation work students in mainline seminaries need if they are to be prepared spiritually for the kind of leadership churches in the twenty-first century need. An elective course or two in a curriculum will not suffice if students are to understand that faith formation and committed discipleship are primary concerns of those who are seeking to educate them for ministry. It is this kind of environment that will encourage and nurture the kind of passion for the gospel on which covenant membership depends and to which it witnesses.

The hope for changing the way we educate ministers lies with faculty and administration. They are the people who set the tone of seminary life. Therefore, they should lead the way. They are the ones who should make sure students understand that the pursuit of knowledge without commensurate commitment to the Christian gospel as the message by which one defines one's life is not worthy of the church's trust. They are the ones whose lives can demonstrate that an educated clergy can love God with heart, head, and hand.

The subject of how poorly seminary education prepared them for the "real" world of the church is common conversation among ministers. To some extent this attitude stems from unrealistic expectations of what seminaries can do. At the same time it also reveals the fact that many of them have become victims of a seminary environment that at best sent them into the church equipped to maintain the status quo. Students and churches need better than this. Clergy are not responsible for all the problems churches face, and seminaries are not the only reason there is ineffective ministerial leadership today. But if clergy are to do more than engage in institutional maintenance or jump on every politically correct bandwagon that rolls by, seminary education will need to take seriously the awesome responsibility of equipping students academically and spiritually for leadership in the church. If faith and theology are to be partners in the church, they must be partners in the education of ministers. Otherwise the church will be led by clergy who know a lot and believe very little or believe a lot and know very little, with communities of faith able to nurture covenant living the casualty of both.

11

Staying in the Church

Some Personal Reflections

Context is important because it shapes how we see things. Where we stand does in fact influence what we see. Let me tell you where I am standing.

Two years ago my wife, Joy, and I made the decision for me to leave a tenured teaching position at a denominational seminary to become co-pastors of a new church start in the Twin Cities area of Minnesota. It is an area where our denomination is virtually unknown. Some friends and colleagues thought it was an exciting opportunity to do what New Testament Christianity is all about—founding churches. Others wondered openly if we had taken leave of our senses, especially at our age! Starting churches is for the young, not middle-aged ministers who are closer to retirement than to their seminary days.

In terms of the growth and strength of our new congregation, as of this writing the future is ultimately in God's hand. In the time we have been here we have learned once again the lesson of scripture that the church's tomorrow is a gift of God. We are doing all we know to do, learning weekly things we had not known before, and are seeing encouraging progress, but when the end of the day comes, we know any security we have is rooted in faith rather than fact.

In the midst of that reality, however, there are some things about which I am absolutely sure. I am more alive spiritually than I have been since being ordained. I am more confident of the truth of Jesus Christ as Savior and Lord than I have ever been. I am more persuaded of the essentialness of the church in living the Christian life than at any time in my ministry. And I am more troubled by the state of the church than I can remember ever being before.

But don't misunderstand. Being "troubled by the state of the church" is to speak as a lover troubled by the behavior of a beloved. Having been either hurt or turned off by the church, there is a strong impulse in people today who claim the label "Christian" to consider the church tangential to their lives. "I guess I should go to church" is a common sentiment among such people, but at the same time they don't see the matter as having any bearing on whether or not they are truly Christian. To a large extent they think this way because they define "Christian" in moralistic terms. Although their standards of morality may differ from that of their parents and grandparents, especially regarding sexual behavior, Baby Boomers and their children still consider moral goodness the key element in what makes a person a Christian. Personal integrity and the way one treats others are likely to be their defining standards. Who really needs the church to practice this kind of morality, especially when so many in the church have shown themselves unable to live this way?

It seems a strange reversal of history that Christians themselves would view the church as an incidental part of the story of God's salvation. It is true that much of what churches do is removed from the simple call to witness to Jesus as Savior and Lord. In my own experience I have seen its humanness firsthand and wondered why it behaves as it so often does. When I hear stories of churches shooting the wounded or spiritually abusing people or standing on the wrong side of moral issues, it is for me, in the words of Yogi Berra, "déjà vu all over again."

But I also know that is not the whole story. When we stay with the church long enough we begin to realize it is more than its sins. It is the community of Jesus Christ. It teaches us the ways of love as much as it contradicts them. Simple people take courageous stands for no other reason than the fact that they are Christian, sacrifice their own comfort and resources to stretch out a helping hand to others, and give hours of labor because they love and are loved by people they call their church family. In our current ministry we are guided by a small group of advisors with whom we meet once a month. Consisting of a few clergy colleagues and laypeople, they serve in this capacity out of a love for Christ and for the church. I have not served with people who better exemplify the best there is about the church.

It is when we are with people such as these that we gain the perspective to realize criticism of the church should be taken seriously only if it comes from love rather than disillusionment. Love for the church cannot be based on one's personal experiences alone. Rather, it must be rooted in the understanding that the church is a community Jesus calls together. He is our bond. When it gathers around the communion table, it is a community of sinners, not saints, expressing gratitude rather than pointing to personal achievements. The church comes to the table as a community of needy people, people who but for the grace of God have no chance to live with the hope of meaningful existence. It comes unworthy of the sacrifice of love it represents, but that's the point. The church comes to the table precisely because it is not good, and certainly not good enough to merit the gift of forgiveness. It comes confessing the guilt of giving into idolatrous ways that betray the very Lord around whose table it gathers.

For reasons we may not fully understand, Jesus has chosen to work through this community of weak, sinful people called the church. This makes belonging to it an absolute necessity for all who follow him. Christian faith cannot be separated from the church. The Westminster Confession of Faith has it right: "There is no ordinary possibility of salvation outside the church." It is not a statement of exclusion, but one that speaks to the power of the Christian community to be an agent for divine love and mercy in spite of its humanness.

So also says Hauerwas, but for different reasons. For him the church is necessary because it is a countercultural movement and as such represents God's political statement of opposition to the dominant culture that wants to claim God's favor but promotes idolatrous living.

> If we say, outside the church there is no salvation, we make a claim about the very nature of salvation—namely that salvation is God's work to restore all creation to the Lordship of Christ. Such a salvation is about the defeat of powers that presume to rule outside God's providential care. Such salvation is not meant to confirm what we already know and/or experience. It is meant to make us part of a story that could not be known apart from exemplification in the lives of people in a concrete community.[41]

I have lived and learned enough through the years to know that being a Christian and being in the church are synonymous states of existence. Scripture is uncompromising in its insistence that being Christian means being a functioning member of the body of Christ. Thus, not being in the church is not an option for the Christian. To say, then, that I am troubled about the state of the church presupposes a deep and unconditional commitment to its life and witness.

Equally important, though, I believe things can be different. That is why this book has been written. But it will take courage for them to be different. Ministers and laity alike will have to make some hard decisions about the nature of the church and the meaning of membership that will not please many in the church. But new life never emerges without struggle and pain. Now is not the time

to cling to things as they have been, but to recognize the new thing
God might now be doing:

> Do not remember the former things,
>   or consider the things of old.
> I am about to do a new thing;
>   now it springs forth, do you not perceive it?
>   (Isa. 43:18–19a)

12

Questions from Ministers
and Laity

Frequently people respond to a new idea by saying, "It sounds good, but I just don't think it will work." In the church this can mean the risk of change is too great, especially when the proposal challenges basic assumptions with which people have lived for years. Or it may be that the minister already feels overloaded with work and has no energy for a new proposal. Whatever the reason, the "good idea" can't work because it doesn't get tried.

The idea for this chapter arose out of a concern that this would be the response to covenant membership. With this in mind I asked several ministers to read the material and raise questions about its practicality. The readers were mainline, ecumenical, diverse in race and gender, ranging in ministry experience from five to more than forty years, and all but one (a denominational staff member) serving in a congregational setting. One shared the material with two groups of laity and included their reactions with her own.

The specific assignment was as follows: "Please raise questions about problems and issues you can anticipate if you were to lead the congregation where you serve to adopt the concept of covenant membership." They understood that their questions and comments, along with my responses, would form the content of this last chapter. Whenever possible I have stated questions as they were received. In a few instances, rewording was necessary to make a question out of a comment or to combine two or more questions about the same issue into one.

The selected readers represent the people who will bear responsibility for showing people a different door through which to enter the church. As is evident from the questions, they took their responsibility seriously. Sometimes the issues they raised led me to rework the material to achieve greater clarity. In the end they were probably more gentle than they needed to be, yet it will be obvious that they did not hesitate to ask tough questions. I am indebted to them for their good work. I am also proud to be one of their colleagues.

+ + +

1. *Why do you think requiring people to be committed will actually "make" them committed?*
   I don't. I am fully aware of the fact that commitment is an inward decision. But standards do help people to know what is expected of them and that often has the effect of encouraging them to live up to them. The best analogy I know to this is the twelve steps of AA. They don't make someone stop drinking, but if a person makes the decision for sobriety the steps provide a practical way to achieve it. Covenant membership expectations, which, by the way, can be defined as a congregation chooses, can help people be faithful to their desire to follow Jesus. They are means to an end, not ends in themselves. This question could be asked of every group or organization. Why have team rules for athletes or club rules for civic organizations? Not to make

people do anything, but to help those who are willing to support the group to know what is involved. The same thing is true with covenant membership.

2. *You make some strong claims for covenant membership. Do you really believe the concept can live up to them, and do you know of any instance where it has been practiced long enough to see the effect you believe it can have?*

I am not sure what specific claims you are referring to. Covenant membership is simply an attempt to make church membership mean commitment to following Jesus by de-emphasizing institutional maintenance and focusing on the gifts and calls to ministry among the laity. In that sense it does offer a significant challenge to the way people now join the church. I tried to say at the beginning of the book that covenant membership will not solve all the problems churches face in regard to nominal commitment, but it is a way for churches to make potential members more aware of what belonging to the church actually involves.

Church of the Savior in Washington, D.C., and Church of the Covenant in Lynchburg, Virginia, are two congregations that have been practicing this approach to membership for more than 50 years. My proposal is somewhat different from what they do, but they have had a significant influence on the way I think about church membership. Both of these churches have remained small but have spawned numerous ministries that continue with great vitality and influence. Each congregation has also been publicly commended by civic leaders in their respective communities for the positive impact they have had in matters related to racial and social justice. Newer congregations that have become what we call megachurches such as Willow Creek Community Church near Chicago and Gingamsburg United Methodist Church near Dayton, Ohio, also have membership requirements. So there is enough history to approaching membership in this way to believe it does help to establish an identity and working ethos within congregational life.

3. *Doesn't covenant membership run the risk of becoming an exclusive club?*

It seems the charge of being "exclusive" comes up whenever a church seeks to impose standards of membership. As I mention in the book, this is one of the criticisms frequently made about Church of the Savior. It's as if people believe there is something wrong with churches' defining what it means to belong to them, yet they support other groups that do precisely the same thing. There isn't much to say except that there is nothing inherent in the concept of covenant membership that would lead a congregation to become intentionally exclusive. There is a lot to prevent this from happening, though. By definition the church does not belong to the members. It belongs to Jesus Christ, which means it is inclusive of everyone who wants to follow him. People may choose to exclude themselves, but covenant membership isn't exclusive just because it has specific requirements.

4. *Over time, why wouldn't covenant membership become institutionalized, as traditional membership now is? In other words, how does covenant membership not become just another church "program"?*

This is always a possibility. People are people. They make mistakes, fail in living up to commitments, and often lose sight of the original purpose of the group to which they belong. Of course, this can happen in a covenant membership church. But the biblical tradition of covenant making serves as a constant source of renewal to keep covenant membership on track. The other thing that limits the possibility of its becoming just another program is its insistence on the ministry of the laity. Programs are clergy dependent, whereas covenant membership is laity dependent. This is a crucial difference. Everything a covenant membership church does should be through its ministry groups, which helps to create a mindset that rejects program-based activities.

5. *If you are really serious about "upping" membership expectations, shouldn't a tithe be the minimum financial commitment?*
Yes, if we follow the biblical tradition. But the issue is not as simple as it may appear to be. By the time an unchurched person or family comes into the church they are sometimes over their heads in debt. This is the reality of living in an age of easy credit, but it also stems from the fact that many of them depended on student loans to get an education. It may take them years to get their heads above water. Tithing is simply not a realistic option for them. What we do at Spirit of Joy is to allow them to establish a lower percentage and commit themselves to raising that a percentage point each year thereafter. For many of these people, giving to the church is a new experience. A percentage less than a tenth is still a significant commitment for them. We see this as a practical way to confront the reality of their situation, which starts them on the road to being good stewards of their resources.

6. *Does the way covenant membership approaches financial stewardship mean annual pledge drives cannot be conducted?*
No, it doesn't interfere with that process at all if that is the way your church approaches budget building. It may be that you will find if you adopt covenant membership you will not need to hold such drives in the future, but that is an issue that has to do with factors other than covenant membership. To answer your specific question, I can say that there is nothing inherent in covenant membership that would prevent you from holding an annual pledge drive.

7. *Doesn't covenant membership still depend on individual conscience in living up to it, and if so, how is this different from traditional membership?*
The answer is yes, but that doesn't mean there is no difference between covenant and traditional church membership. No

approach to membership, whether in the church or some other organization, can eliminate the fact that individuals ultimately decide whether or nor to live up to commitments they make. We wouldn't want it any other way. A commitment wouldn't mean much if we had no choice about it. In this regard, both approaches to church membership agree. The difference lies in the fact that the traditional approach leaves it up to the individual to determine what membership means, whereas the congregation makes this decision in covenant membership. The reason for this is that covenant membership trusts the group to determine the meaning of membership based on its understanding of scripture and the internal needs of the community rather than letting each person decide that on his or her own. The difference may seem minor, but in practice it is huge.

8. *Doesn't annual recommitment encourage people to think of church membership as their decision alone and no one else's? That is, doesn't it breed the attitude you are trying to overcome— that membership is an individual choice?*

As I just said, we are never going to stop people from thinking for themselves, nor do we want to. I don't see how annual recommitment pushes them further in this direction. All it does is to get them to think about their commitment to church membership on an annual basis. It is a consciousness-raising process, if nothing else, especially when it is done in a worship setting. Once my home church held a service and invited all married couples to reaffirm their vows. I was a teenager at the time, but it made a lasting impression on me, and I suspect it did for all those couples. I just don't see the problem you do in having a regular time to reaffirm our commitment to church membership. I can also think of some legitimate reasons why a person would not feel ready to recommit in a given year, but would again at a later time. In a real sense this would be nothing more than acknowledging what would have probably already taken place inwardly. If people drop out and in when it comes to genuine commitment to the church, why not give them a formal way to do that?

9. *How do you determine when a person is not keeping covenant, and what do you do about it?*
   Most of the elements of our particular covenant pledge at Spirit of Joy are the kind that make assessment easy—attendance in worship, financial giving, and participation in ministry. At the same time, things such as daily prayer and Bible reading or involvement in an individual ministry we may not know about have to be left to individual conscience. It helps that we talk about covenant constantly. Should Joy and I become aware of someone who was obviously not keeping covenant, we would make a pastoral call to see if there was a problem with which we could be of some help. In the future the issue of accountability will be handled by a ministry group within the congregation. It is, after all, a community issue, and the community should have some way of confronting it.

10. *How do you deal with the fact that potential members are at such different places in their spiritual journey?*
    This is something any approach to membership faces. Covenant membership recognizes that equally committed Christian people can have different attitudes about membership requirements. A covenant membership church is simply asking everyone to think about the good of the whole body. At the same time, it must communicate clearly that membership is not a requisite for participation in church life. In this way a covenant membership church tries to support people wherever they may be spiritually while asking them to support the need for a common commitment among those who choose to be members.

    More than anything else, what helps the most is for people to live with a community for a while before joining. Some of us at Spirit of Joy worshiped together for more than a year before we began membership. During this time we were able to get to know one another and to discern if covenant membership was a commitment we could or wanted to make. We think that's a good model for everyone. A person can participate fully in the life of the church without joining. All we're saying is that we want people to know the community and what is expected of them as members before they join.

11. *How do you tell people who have been members for years who resist covenant membership they cannot be members any longer?*
You don't, of course. Lopping off people from the membership roll will serve no good purpose. Established churches will have to ask for voluntary commitment to the covenant from existing members without even a hint at removing them from the roll if they do not make covenant. I don't see it as having a double standard to do this while making covenant a requirement for new members. I mention in the book that I am aware of one church that is approaching it this way. It's the only way it can be done that doesn't lead to a conflict that would defeat the purpose of moving in this direction. Over time, current members will see the value of covenant for the congregation as a whole and become supporters of it. I would say that within five years existing members refusing to make covenant would no longer be an issue.

12. *Doesn't covenant membership imply that those who do not make covenant stand outside salvation?*
Absolutely not. Membership has to do with what is called *ecclesiology.* That is, it has to do with what it means to be the church. Salvation is a theological issue that has to do with God's relationship to humanity. The two are obviously related but speak to very different issues and needs. So being or not being a covenant member is not an issue of salvation. But let me go a step further. I say in the book that I believe being a Christian means being in the church, that is, being

a participant in the community of faith called the body of Christ. But this doesn't mean you have to put your name on the church roll. The New Testament describes Christians as followers of "the Way," not church members. Covenant membership isn't an attempt to pass judgment on whether or not someone is a "true" Christian, or even a good or bad church member. It is a practical way to help churches fulfill the responsibility of spelling out what church membership means in more detail. This has nothing to do with the matter of salvation.

13. *How does covenant membership help children understand discipleship?*
The short answer is by modeling what it means to follow Jesus. Children need to know they are part of the church even if they are not members. By talking about the meaning of covenant membership in language they can understand, children will learn about it, but we do more than talk. We engage them in activities that teach them about the elements of our covenant pledge. For example, they decide among choices we give them how their church school offering will be used. They also take up the Blessings Quarters offering we collect during the worship service consisting of quarters that symbolize the blessings of the week. This money is used to bless the lives of people outside our immediate fellowship. Something we do that is particular to us is that we have a time for the children to receive communion. The Lord's supper is part of our weekly worship. The first service we held, the children unexpectedly came forward with their parents for communion. The next week we had them out of the service during this time. During the fellowship hour one of our five-year-olds approached Joy and said she wanted some bread. Thinking she was referring to the banana bread made for fellowship time, Joy pointed her to where it was. Calista immediately began to cry. Her mother came over and told Joy she thought what Calista really wanted was the

communion bread. Joy went to get it, and Calista took a small piece. Then she pointed to the cup. As Joy placed it in front of her, she started to dip the bread in the cup, paused, and said to Joy, "Say those words to me you said last week." That is how sharing communion with our children got started. It clearly meant something to Calista to share in it the week before. We were confident the others felt the same way. Of course, they cannot understand its full meaning. We often tell them they will have to decide when they are older if they want to be baptized and continue to take communion. But for now it is one way we believe we can teach them about the love of God that is the basis for our covenant with one another and also make them feel they are important members of our community of faith now. Other things can be done, but the point is that we are intentional in trying to teach our children what covenant community is.

14. *How do church traditions that extend an invitation to membership at the end of a worship service practice covenant membership?*

This question is important for Spirit of Joy because in the Disciples tradition we extend such an invitation. What we do is to invite people who know about and understand the covenant commitment they will make to come forward to be recognized and sign the covenant. At the same time we ask those who do not know about covenant membership to consider enrolling in the next class that will be held to explain what it is about. Should someone who has been baptized come forward unexpectedly, we would ask them to renew their profession of faith, but we would wait until they have completed the membership class before receiving them into covenant. If an unbaptized person were to come forward, we would receive their profession of faith and baptize them but still expect them to take the membership class before joining.

15. *Are you making a distinction between uniting with the church as the body of Christ and joining a congregation?*
The answer is both yes and no. Yes in terms of saying a person can be a member of the universal church, that is, the body of Christ, but cannot join our congregation until they complete the covenant membership class and say they will seek to be faithful to the covenant pledge. No in terms of our congregation's being a part of the larger body of Christ in the world, so that to be a member of Spirit of Joy makes one a member of the universal church. Let me make clear that I am not saying only a covenant membership church is the real body of Christ. I don't believe that for a minute. We are all in the body wherever we might belong as long as we have made a sincere commitment to following Jesus.

16. *How do you determine if a person is ready to become a covenant member?*
We don't. That is a decision the person makes, and we accept it at face value. Let me add that we do spend time talking to our teenagers about how they can live up to the covenant pledge. We have found that they are not always clear about how to do that at this point in their lives, especially the element of financial support or serving in a ministry, yet they want to be members of the church. It's up to us to help them figure out how they can take the covenant seriously.

17. *Isn't this approach more suited to new churches than established ones?*
No. The gospel needs to challenge the idolatry of the dominant culture, and the hope for that cannot be limited to new churches. To begin with, there just are not enough of them, but the issue really has to do with the integrity of church membership, and that certainly has to do with established churches. If you're asking if covenant membership has a better chance of being accepted in a new church, the answer is probably yes. But even then there are risks involved. The need for people in new churches, especially those that

start with no core group as ours did, is acute. Spelling out expectations for membership runs the risk of losing some of the few you have. Also, some new churches are satellites from existing congregations with as many as a hundred people to start with. That means they already have traditions to confront similar to an established church. It is true that new ideas often do get a hearing easier in a new church, but that doesn't mean they are easily embraced. Covenant membership is for every church, and at the same time every church—new or old—will be stretched in uncomfortable ways by it.

18. *Doesn't "nominal" membership sometimes help people ease back into church life, especially when they have been previously hurt by the church?*
    I don't see how nominal membership helps someone ease back into church life. I'm not even sure what that means. If you are talking about giving people "space" so they can get their feet under them because of a personal trauma or a bad experience in another church, I think participation without membership will do this. The good thing about annual membership is that by its very nature it says that participation without membership does not place a person outside the fellowship of the community. We emphasize the freedom of people to say no to membership in order to be truly free to say yes. I would think someone who needed to be in church with no expectations on them would respond to this kind of freedom in a positive way.
    Maybe what you are thinking in suggesting that nominal membership can help a person ease back into church life is that it allows them to be a member without getting involved. Again, I don't see how that helps anything. At some point they will still have to decide to make a commitment or stay a spectator. Covenant membership allows for both, but in my opinion does so in a way that is much more defined and helpful than nominal membership does.

19. *What are the specific steps established churches can take to move to covenant membership?*

I have already mentioned that the minister(s) will need to teach and preach about the biblical basis of covenant. It is especially important to have membership classes for new people so they can understand fully what covenant membership means. Holding such classes in an established church for existing members can also be helpful. Working with current lay leadership groups such as elders, deacons, or congregational officers is absolutely essential. Further, involving the governing body in actually writing the covenant pledge can be an important way to get them to support it.

In one congregation where we served, we began an annual covenant renewal worship service as a way to highlight the kind of commitment church membership should represent. We distributed covenant symbols (which we are also doing at Spirit of Joy) and asked members to keep them in a prominent place during the year to remind them of their covenant with the church. It was a voluntary thing. No one was under pressure to take a symbol or even to participate in the unison reading of the covenant. This service began to hold great meaning for the vast majority of the people in that church.

One thing to remember is that this process cannot be rushed or circumvented. We spent a year talking about the nature of the church and the call to ministry for everyone as a way of preparing our congregation for this way of receiving members. Our first covenant membership Sunday was the week after Easter, so we spent the entire Lenten season focusing on the obstacles to covenant discussed in chapter 6. Our newsletter, which is focused more on education than promotion, had numerous articles on the meaning of covenant membership over a number of months.

In an established church this kind of process would be even more crucial. Communication is one of the keys. People will have less anxiety about covenant membership the more they know about it. Moreover, there are many current church members who are living out their relationship to the church in a covenantal way already. They will become the ambassadors to help others come on board.

Prayer retreats can also be of immense help in moving a church toward covenant. They allow the Spirit to work in small groups, which then become leaven in the whole loaf. When people are growing spiritually, they are much more open to new ideas and concepts even if they make them uncomfortable.

One final thing I would say is don't put this thing to a vote. Take as long as it takes to get a consensus around the concept. Ask everyone to be open and honest in seeking a consensus and then trust the Spirit to create it. Voting on it will never do. That is not the way to make decisions in the church on anything as far as I am concerned, but certainly not on covenant membership. No one can make a church into a covenant membership congregation.

20. *What are some "must do's" for ministers in leading a church to adopt covenant membership? In other words, what is the most important role clergy can play in this process?*

Besides what I have already said about teaching and preaching, there is the need for the minister to balance strength of conviction with pastoral sensitivity. Both require a lot of time spent in prayer and Bible reading. There is no shortcut to having the spiritual reserves to lead a church through significant change. The minister also needs to have an unshakable sense of having been called to be where he or she is serving in ministry. This sense of call gets you through the tough times when nothing else does.

Whenever any new idea is presented that has the potential for resistance, pastoral care becomes all the more important. My sense is that any change that clergy advocate goes down better when people know they can express disagreement without the minister's getting angry with them. Sometimes they are not able to extend the same courtesy to the minister. When this happens, there is no choice but to treat them as one would like to be treated, pray for them, but also hold firm to the goal toward which you are trying to lead the church. Leadership is easy when everyone is in agreement, but the real test is to stay the course when things get tense. That takes inward strength.

Related to something I said earlier, seek out a group of lay leaders to work with as you lead the church into covenant membership. It may be an established group such as elders, deacons, a pastoral relations group, or a governing body. You will need their support on a personal level as well as for the proposal to be accepted by the congregation as a whole. The important thing is not to do this alone.

21. *Doesn't covenant membership create tension with denominations that measure success for churches and ministers statistically?*
Probably, but who cares? I'm not trying to be curt or cute. My response is a serious one. Ministers who care about statistical success that denominational officials will applaud won't be interested in covenant membership in the first place, so it's really a non-issue. Those who think covenant membership has potential don't need denominational approval to feel that they are successful. Competent ministers know success in ministry, whether in a large or a small church, is more accurately determined by their faithfulness to the gospel's call to holiness, devotion, and justice seeking.

Having said that, I want to add that the regional church that has sponsored our new church start has actually been quite supportive of covenant membership. Our regional minister and president participated in our first covenant service and has spoken positively about it to other groups. Numerical measurements are part of denominational life, and the pressure must be enormous on executives to play the game. Yet there are leaders who have been able to resist complete capitulation to measuring success in this way.

One last thought on this question. Covenant membership is part of an overall change in the way churches understand themselves and go about ministry. This conflicts with the fact that most denominational offerings presuppose the status quo, such as traditional women's and men's groups and the functional committee organizational pattern (an oxymoron, in my opinion). At Spirit of Joy we have none of this. This means that when we go to a denominational event we are likely to get very little help with how we actually approach ministry. This makes us reluctant to take the time or spend the money to attend such meetings. That can create tension, but under the circumstances I don't know how to avoid it.

22. *Since any talk of membership, even covenant membership, will allow the demon of institutionalization to get its foot in the door, why not go a step farther and simply stop talking about membership at all?*
    It's a point well taken. I don't see how membership actually serves the cause of Christ much. Twelve-step groups don't have members, just participants, and they are flourishing at a time when mainline churches are declining. That suggests the bonds of community consist of a lot more than a membership roll. At the same time, covenant membership can serve the same function as a legal marriage does. It is a public declaration of mutual trust and commitment, and people choose to take this step when they could simply live together. That tells me there is something within the human spirit that needs some kind of formal acknowledgment of the bonding that occurs between people. In the end, though, I suppose it comes down to whether or not eliminating membership altogether is a battle—and it would be—worth fighting. Right now I don't think it is.

23. *Is the "prescription" strong enough to overcome the problem?*
    This is similar question to the previous one, but also goes to a slightly different issue. The problem with church membership today is not simply some people's lack of commitment. That will always be a problem because people are human. The problem covenant membership addresses has to do with the church's easy tolerance of nominal

membership without realizing the negative impact it has on the church's life and witness. In this sense I believe covenant membership is a "prescription" strong enough to overcome the problem. Problems will arise that are particular to covenant membership, but the fact that it has specific expectations stated up front provides a point of reference to which a church can appeal when confronting them. What I am saying, in essence, is that covenant membership does adequately address the problem it seeks to solve.

Notes

[1]Stanley Hauerwas and William H. Willimon, *Resident Aliens* (Nashville: Abingdon Press, 1989).

[2]H. Richard Niebuhr, *Christ and Culture* (New York: Harper & Brothers, 1951).

[3]Jan G. Linn, *The Jesus Connection* (St. Louis: Chalice Press, 1997).

[4]Jan G. Linn, *Reclaiming Evangelism: A Practical Guide For Mainline Churches* (St. Louis: Chalice Press, 1998).

[5]Robert Bellah, Richard Madsen, William M. Sullivan, Ann Swidler, and Steven M. Tipton, *Habits of the Heart* (San Francisco: Harper & Row, 1985), 142.

[6]Ibid.

[7]Luke Timothy Johnson, *Living Jesus: Learning the Heart of the Gospel* (San Francisco: Harper San Francisco, 1999).

[8]From Edythe Draper, *Draper's Book of Quotations for the Christian World* (Wheaton, Ill.: Tyndale House, Parson's Quick Verse, 5th ed.), #11322.

[9]Jim Cymbala and Dean Merrill, *Fresh Wind, Fresh Fire* (Grand Rapids, Mich.: Zondervan, 1998), 73.

[10]Ibid., 83.

[11]Ibid., 128–29.

[12]Jan G. Linn, *What Ministers Wish Church Members Knew* (St. Louis: Chalice Press, 1994).

[13]Douglas John Hall, *The Steward: A Biblical Symbol Come of Age* (Grand Rapids: Eerdmans, 1990), 244.

[14]Statistics taken from *Year Book & Directory 1999* of the Christian Church (Disciples of Christ).

[15]Ibid.

[16]Bill Hull, *Can the Evangelical Church Be Saved?* (Grand Rapids, Mich.: Fleming H. Revell, 1993), 8.

[17]From a sermon delivered at the National Evangelistic Association of the Christian Church (Disciples of Christ) meeting in Cincinnati, Ohio, in October 1999.

[18]From a lecture delivered in April 2000 at Luther Theological Seminary, St. Paul, Minnesota.

[19]Dietrich Bonhoeffer, *The Cost of Discipleship* (New York: MacMillan, 1963), 47.

[20]Ibid., 99.

[21]Ibid., 68.

[22]Original source untraced.

[23]Christopher Levan, *The Dancing Steward* (Toronto: The United Church Publishing House, 1993), 15.

[24]David Gibson, "Study finds younger Jews redefining their faith," Minneapolis Star-Tribune, 15 July 2000.

[25]Ibid.

[26]James A. Sanders, *From Sacred Story to Sacred Text* (Philadelphia: Fortress Press, 1987), 19.

[27]Allen Gibson, Senior Minister, Aldersgate United Methodist Church, Louisville, Ky. From daily reflections he sends to friends via e-mail.

[28]Alvin Toffler, *Future Shock* (New York: Bantam Books, 1971).

[29]Ibid., 326.

[30]Ibid., 20.

[31]Ibid., 186.

[32]Ibid., 358–61.

[33]Ibid., 258.

[34]*Affluenza*, co-produced by KCTS/Seattle and Oregon Public Broadcasting, 1997.

[35]Henri J. M. Nouwen, *Sabbatical Journey: The Diary of His Final Year* (New York: Crossroad, 1998), 16.

[36]Bryan P. Stone, *Compassionate Ministry: Theological Foundations* (Maryknoll, N.Y.: Orbis Books, 1996), 52.

[37]Hauerwas and Willimon, *Resident Aliens*, 43.

[38]Ellen Goodman, "Creationism vs. evolution met with a hearty 'whatever,'" *Minneapolis Star-Tribune*, 16 March 2000.

[39]Nouwen, *Sabbatical Journey,* 156.

[40]Goodman, "Creationism vs. Evolution."

[41]Stanley Hauerwas, *After Christendom? How the Church Is to Behave If Freedom, Justice and a Christian Nation Are Bad Ideas* (Nashville: Abingdon Press, 1991), 37.